Geor

First Guardian of American Liberty

By Michael Crawley

Table of Contents

Introduction

Every person in America—or at least, everyone who stayed awake during their history classes in high school—thinks they know who George Washington was. What can you recall about him right off the top of your head? You probably remember that he was the first President of the United States, and that he commanded the American army against the British forces during the Revolutionary War. You may also have a vague recollection of a children's fable about George Washington chopping down a cherry tree, or flinging a silver dollar across a river. The precise details of Washington's military accomplishments and political endeavors, however, are facts that you've probably forgotten over the years, unless you have made a point of studying him in greater depth.

Despite the fact that the average person has forgotten most of what they ever knew about

George Washington, most Americans nonetheless cherish the belief that he was a good man—perhaps unrealistically good, as if he were carved from the same stone as the monument that bears his name. Of all the American founders, Washington's legacy seems to have suffered the least tarnish over the centuries. We see the famous paintings of Washington praying at Valley Forge, or standing at the prow of the boat that made the Delaware crossing, and find that our idea of who Washington was differs little in the particulars from these idealized images. We are content to see him as stoic, courageous, unselfish, and unambitious, as though his imagined goodness is a reflection on the character of the nation he helped to build.

The life of any person who has been mythologized to the extent that Washington's has is bound to contain surprises that contradict our popular notion of their character. This is just as likely to be true of history's most beloved figures as it is to be true of its most reviled ones.

It discomfits us now when confronted with evidence that, for instance, Hitler was fond of dogs; we are invested in the idea of Hitler as a man so evil that no ordinary human can relate to him on any level. We are similarly discomfited by any hint of moral grayness in a man we uphold as a paragon. Take, for example, the popular American view on Washington and slavery.

The fact that Washington was a slave-holder is incontrovertible, but we still seem to have difficulty holding it in mind. This is partly due to our own modern reluctance to address the subject of slavery and its implications in our own time. Studying the eighteenth century, the modern reader encounters so many matter of fact references to slave ownership that the effect can be disconcerting, as it almost creates the impression that the authors of such histories have set aside their awareness that slavery was a systematic atrocity. But such references are vital to understanding the financial situations of persons such as Washington. The wealth of eighteenth century persons is less often reckoned in terms of a yearly income and more often stated in terms of the number of acres of land they owned, and the number of slaves. The worth of a slave was roughly equivalent to the worth of a new car in the twenty first century. Once you have grasped this, you are better equipped to understand how invested land owners in particular were in maintaining the institution of slavery. The agrarian economy of the south, where Washington lived, was utterly dependent on slaves, and the wealth of plantation owners was accrued through their unpaid labor.

Whenever Washington's ownership of slaves is referred to, it is invariably followed by the hasty reminder that he freed all of his own slaves in his will after his death. We dispense with any examination of the fact that Washington acquired a number of slaves over his lifetime in addition to those he inherited. While he developed increasingly favorable feelings towards the cause of abolition over his lifetime, he did not transcend the morality of his social class and his era to any considerable degree until the very end of his life. Washington was no worse than most wealthy Virginian planters, and more liberal than some—the fact that he did free his slaves in will was a remarkable deed for his era. But the fact that he freed his slaves when he died seems to be easier for many of us to remember than the fact he went to considerable lengths to prevent his slaves from taking advantage of opportunities to gain their freedom legally, or that he vigorously pursued slaves who ran away.

Americans see their country as the birthplace of freedom, indeed, as almost originating the concept of a free citizenry governed by the people. American nationalism is wrapped up in a myth of divine blessing and goodness. In some ways, it is as if we need to believe that the man we regard as the "Father of His Country" was almost a saint. That is to say, we have little sense of his true personality, and this makes him an invitingly blank canvas against which to project our own wish-fulfilling conjectures about his character.

While Washington may not have actively tried to make anyone believe that he was a saint or a paragon, some of his most famous biographers do consider him responsible for having deliberately made himself difficult to know. According to historian Ron Chernow, Washington "wanted the public to know him as a public man, concerned with the public weal and transcending egotistical needs." In other words, he considered it part of his service to the country to let his actions speak for him and let the people make of him what they chose.

In some ways, the image most people have of Washington now says more about what Americans wish the first president of their country to have been than about any pressing curiosity to know who he was in truth. In recent years, however, a large number of Washington's personal correspondence and papers have come to light, and as a result it is more possible to gain an understanding of his motivations and feelings than in former decades. Scholarship on George Washington has consequently entered a new age.

This book does not aim to compete with serious academic scholarship about Washington or the events that shaped his life, but rather to serve as a gateway to such scholarship for the casual reader who may be interested in acquiring a basic understanding of the facts of his biography. It condenses the findings of a number of lengthier and more in-depth sources, with as much reference as possible in the limitations of space to primary sources.

We will begin by covering the early years of Washington's childhood, his education, his teenage years as a surveyor in Virginia, and the beginning of his military career as an officer of the Virginia militia and an aide to a general in the British army. Since American history courses generally begin with the years leading up to the

American Revolution, this will provide the reader with some interesting context for the decades prior, when America was still a prosperous British colony chiefly concerned with conflicts over land with the French and the Native Americans. In later chapters, we will examine how Washington achieved tremendous wealth as a planter, aided greatly by his marriage to Martha Custis, a wealthy widow, and how his rising status as one of the most prominent planters in Virginia brought him into conflict with British taxation policies, and cemented his conviction that America's separation from Britain was necessary. The second half of the book will cover Washington's service as a Virginia delegate to the Constitutional Congress, his appointment as Commander in Chief of the Continental Army, and the two terms he served as the first president of the United States before voluntarily stepping down and retiring to his home at Mount Vernon.

A book of this length can hope to do little more than establish a very broad outline of the most interesting and relevant facts about Washington's life and career. However, if you have little more familiarity with Washington's story other than the basics that are covered in a typical U.S. history class in high school, this book should expose you to some new perspectives and hopefully whet your appetite for longer volumes that dwell on the fascinating richness of Washington's correspondences, his vision for the United States during the first years of the early republic, and his relationships with other compelling figures of the eighteenth century.

Any such examination of a popular and highly venerated figure from history must effectively brush away some of the glitter from their memory, in an effort to delineate the rougher, less refined, and more human characteristics of the living person who gave rise to the legend. Such an examination is not conducted with pejorative intentions. George Washington has been elevated to the status of a hero, and anything that is inconsistent with our image of what a hero should be has been elided from the legends surrounding him. Therefore, the effort of historians to restore his human complexity may feel like an attempt to tear a national monument down off its pedestal.

But no act of desecration is intended; the founders of the United States were, like all people in all eras, products of their times. If it is difficult to reconcile our image of a man like Washington with certain brutal realities, it is as well to remember that our own notions of what is moral, honorable, and humane may be judged differently by our own descendants, who have had the benefit of our failures to serve as an example. And by remembering the historical context of the times Washington lived in, we can better appreciate the genuine acts of heroism he was responsible for, though they may differ from those previously attributed to him when our perspective was more limited.

Because the history that is passed down to us can never be more than a subjective effort at representing the truth, it is essential for even the most casual student of history to consult primary sources whenever possible. For this reason, sample extracts from pertinent documents had been reproduced throughout this book, and links to the complete sources are found in the "Primary Sources" guide at the end.

Chapter One: The Early Years 1732-1753

The Washington Family

By the time of George Washington's birth to Mary and Augustine Washington on February 22, 1732, the Washington family had been resident in the American colony of Virginia for nearly eighty years. His great-grandfather, an Englishman named John Washington, settled in Virginia in 1657, after John's father, an Oxford educated Church of England clergyman, suffered a disastrous reversal of fortunes during the English Civil War, when Oliver Cromwell deposed Charles I and instituted a brief republic. John amassed considerable acreage in Virginia, which his son Lawrence, and grandson Augustine, would expand even further.

Contrary to common belief, George Washington was not born into the uppermost echelons of Virginia planter society. Augustine Washington was well off, but not fantastically wealthy; he owned several small tobacco farms, the chief of which, Ferry Farm, was George's home until he was eight years old. The Washingtons were prosperous landed gentry and slave-holders who held a variety of public offices in Virginia and expanded their social standing through marriage and military service. But the enormous wealth and pre-eminent standing in Virginia society that George Washington is known for was attained through, among other things, the patronage of powerful mentors, a highly advantageous marriage, and canny land purchases.

The large amount of land owned by the Washingtons reflected the needs of the tobacco farmer. In the primary tobacco-growing regions of the United States, such as Virginia and North Carolina, the soil is a dense red clay, and tobacco is one of few crops which has a root system strong enough to penetrate it. However, tobacco wears out the soil; each successive years' crop is poorer than the last. Crop rotation, the practice of growing different plant crops in turn in order to replenish the soil's nutrients, was only just beginning to be practiced in the eighteenth century; George Washington would avail himself of this modern technique, but Augustine Washington, like other tobacco farmers of his day, was forced to acquire more and more land in order to grow successful crops in soil that could sustain them.

When Augustine died in 1743, he left behind 10,000 acres, which were divided between his three surviving sons; George inherited Ferry Farm and 10 slaves. Interestingly, the large estate along the Potomac River which Lawrence Washington inherited, and which George would later inherit from him, was the home which is so famously associated with Washington today: Mount Vernon. Lawrence, a captain in the British army, named his estate after Admiral Edward Vernon, his commanding officer in the War of Jenkin's Ear.

Education

"In the Presence of Others Sing not to yourself with a humming Noise, nor Drum with your Fingers or Feet.

If You Cough, Sneeze, Sigh, or Yawn, do it not Loud but Privately; and Speak not in your Yawning, but put Your handkerchief or Hand before your face and turn aside.

Sleep not when others Speak, Sit not when others stand, Speak not when you Should hold your Peace, walk not on when others Stop.

Put not off your Cloths in the presence of Others, nor go out your Chamber half Dressed."

Extract, *Principles of Civility*, 1695

Both Augustine and Mary Washington were married and widowed before they were married to each other. Augustine had two sons who survived to adulthood by his first wife, Jane; these were George's half brothers, Augustine and Lawrence. George was one of seven children born to Augustine and Mary, five of whom, including George, survived to adulthood. The elder Augustine Washington died when George was 11. He was left in the care of his mother, with whom he had a bitterly conflicted relationship. However, his half brother Lawrence, who was fourteen years older than George, acted as a substitute father and mentor, and went to considerable lengths to assist George's career as best he could despite the obstacles that Mary Washington put in his path. His father, grandfather, and so many of his siblings died young that by the time George reached young adulthood, he had conceived the idea that his own lifetime would be short as well, and that it was the more important to make the best possible use of his short time on earth.

The early death of his father and his mother's somewhat inexplicable indifference to his preferences conspired to rob the young George Washington of the formal education he ought to have received. Boys of his social class were expected to be educated along classical lines; his brothers Augustine and Lawrence had both been sent to school in England at about the age George was when his father died. But Mary Washington, who, somewhat contrary to the custom of the time, chose to remain a prosperous widow rather than remarry and hand the management of her estates to a new husband, expected George to take up the duties of his father in caring for their properties. Mary Washington's mother had been illiterate, and her own surviving letters contain poor spelling and grammar, which suggest that she herself was not well educated; some scholars believe this was responsible for the low priority she placed on formal schooling, although she read aloud to the family in the evenings from morally instructive religious tomes.

Details about George's intermittent schooling are scant and difficult to verify. He may have received instruction from tutors and village schools until he was about fifteen, but the majority of his education was probably derived from a program of self-directed reading in the time he could spare from managing his family's estates. Everything he could teach himself from books by diligent study, such as correct penmanship and advanced mathematics, he learned assiduously, but he deeply felt his lack of a classical education. Famously, as a boy Washington copied out lessons from a seventeenth century French guide to polite behavior, entitled *Principles of Civility,* a list of rules governing almost every imaginable aspect of a young man's life and relationships with others. Washington seems to have studied this list very attentively.

The lessons George taught to himself were largely practical in nature: geometry, measurements, law, economics, and rudiments of surveying, all of which stood him in good stead as he attempted to fulfill the functions of an adult in managing his family's properties. His lack of attainments such as Latin, Greek, and

French, set him apart from highly educated people like John Adams, Thomas Jefferson, and Alexander Hamilton, with whom he would form the government of the new nation; as a result, some of them considered him too illiterate for his high office, despite the fact that he was highly intelligent. His sense of inferiority over his lack of education led him to value education highly in others and stress its importance to the young people he would be a mentor and guardian to later in his life.

Washington's Mentors: Lawrence Washington and William Fairfax

The young George Washington's desire for self improvement led him to model himself closely on his brother Lawrence, whose European education, military experience, and general air of glamor captivated George's imagination in a profound way. Lawrence's wife Ann was the daughter of one of the most powerful people in colonial Virginia: William Fairfax, cousin of the

English baron Thomas, Lord Fairfax, represented his kinsman's interests in the New World. The Fairfaxes controlled 5 million acres of land and were spectacularly wealthy. As a result, when Lawrence Washington married into the family, he promptly rose to the very highest levels of Virginia society.

Lawrence lived at the Fairfax estate, Belvoir, which was quite near Mount Vernon, and he made a particular point of inviting his younger brother George to visit him as often as possible, as a means of getting him away from his mother's control. Lawrence's father in law William Fairfax became particularly fond of George during these visits, during which they read and discussed books and such topics as how a young man should deport himself in civilized society. Fairfax, perceiving unusual ability and drive in George, stepped into the role of a patron to him, an act of benevolence which had an incalculably valuable effect on Washington's later career. Not only was George exposed to a world of social refinement and important political connections at Belvoir; simply put, without the backing of a man so considerably above his own station, none of the achievements for which Washington is famous today would have been within his grasp.

Fairfax's first attempt to secure the young Washington's future, undertaken at Lawrence's urging, involved a bid to enlist George in the royal navy. George was interested in pursuing this opportunity, mostly because Lawrence recommended it, but he required his mother's permission, as he was only fourteen at the time. Mary Washington agreed to the plan at first, but after seeking the advice of her brother, ultimately refused her permission. She was told that colonial officers faced a good deal of prejudice in the British military, and that George would find it difficult to advance to a high rank; the truth of this would become manifest to George in later years, when he was consistently denied a royal commission in the Virginia militia. The next year, when George was fifteen, the family faced a severe financial crisis. Washington, who excelled in mathematics and had been left a complete set of surveying tools by his father, determined to embark on a career as a surveyor.

Washington the Surveyor

Surveying was a crucial task in America during the eighteenth century, when so much land was yet unsettled. It involved the use of compasses and geometric calculations and telescopic lenses to calculate boundary lines between properties. As a planter who was responsible for thousands of acres, Washington had some practice in surveying already; he knew the importance of establishing precise legal boundaries between his own lands and those of his neighbors. Boundary lines were particularly important when it came to the sale of land. Most of the 5 million acres controlled by the Fairfax family needed to be divided into plots before it could be sold.

Surveyors made excellent money, and, more importantly from Washington's point of view, they were in a better position than anyone else in colonial Virginia to discover which were the best parcels of land to purchase for themselves. Throughout his life, Washington would be an enthusiastic purchaser of land, acquiring tens of thousands of acres in Virginia and the Ohio Country.

In 1749, when George Washington was 17, William Fairfax appointed him as a county surveyor—a position he could only have obtained through patronage, as he was the youngest surveyor in the history of Virginia and had little practical experience to justify such an appointment. A year later, having made enough money to give up his official position, Washington started working on his own as a surveyor of the lands administered by the Northern Neck Land Office. He made an expedition into the public lands of what was then the American frontier—the unsettled territory west of Virginia, extending to the Ohio and Mississippi rivers. These years of frontier surveying involved a sharp change from the refined lifestyle Washington had been accustomed to at Belvoir—he slept on the ground and cooked meat on sticks over open fires, wearing the same clothes daily and hunting to survive. But Washington's love of the land ran deeply enough that he thrived on the rough outdoor work. In 1750 alone, he made forty-seven surveys, and made his first land purchase, a tract which spanned 1500 acres in the Shenandoah Valley.

Death of Lawrence Washington

In 1749, Lawrence Washington began exhibiting signs of tuberculosis, which in the eighteenth century was invariably a deadly disease. He was forced to quit his seat in the House of Burgesses, the governing body of colonial Virginia, and sail to England to consult with doctors there. George Washington was distressed by this, but he was unable to accompany Lawrence to England or visit his sister in law Ann at Mount Vernon because he himself was suffering from malaria. Lawrence returned from England without having been cured of his illness. His next attempt at treatment was a visit to the site of a natural hot spring in what is now West Virginia. George accompanied Lawrence on the West Virginia trip, then in 1751 to Barbados, where he contracted smallpox. George returned to Virginia after his recovery, while Lawrence went to Bermuda. But neither Barbados nor Bermuda provided Lawrence with the hoped-for cure, and he died shortly after his return to Virginia in 1752.

Washington was understandably devastated by the death of a brother he had looked up to as a second father, but his inheritance from Lawrence would greatly increase his material wealth; according to the terms of Lawrence's will, Mount Vernon, though belonging to Ann Washington in her lifetime, would pass to George when she died. But George would seek to fill his brother's shoes in other ways as well. Lawrence's death left vacant the position of adjutant general, or commander of the Virginia militia; Lawrence had been a soldier deployed in the War of Jenkin's Ear against the Spanish at Cartagena, and had been given a royal commission. George, on the other hand, had no military experience whatsoever and was only 21 years old, but when Lawrence's old adjutant position was split into four district adjutant positions, George lobbied all of his considerably powerful political connections in order to be awarded the most prestigious of them.

Washington's desire to be appointed to the post of district adjutant for the Northern Neck district of Virginia was directly inspired by Lawrence's death, as if Washington believed that by emulating his brother's career he could preserve something of his life. It is not certain whether he previously possessed any military ambitions other than those Lawrence had encouraged in attempting to send him into the navy at the age of 14. However, the timing of Lawrence's death, and thus of the beginning of Washington's military career, coincided with rising hostilities on the American frontier between British and French soldiers. Washington's considerable experience navigating the American wilderness as a surveyor recommended him where his lack of military experience failed to do so. When the French and Indian War, or the Seven Years War as it was known in Europe, broke out in 1754, Washington would not only be on the front lines—his actions would be directly responsible for provoking the conflict.

Chapter Two: A Young Officer 1753-1758

"While in others of [Washington's] extreme youth the years may have implied limitations in the expectations focused upon his endeavors, this never seemed to be considered in respect to the tasks put upon his shoulders."

Valley Forge Historical Society, 1966

The Ohio Company

In the region west of the thirteen settled American colonies lay vast tracts of land, inhabited by Native Americans, but regarded by the colonial European powers as the rightful property of whichever nation could hold it. This region was known as the Ohio Country, and in the Virginia frontier to the north and west of the Ohio River, the land was administered for sale and settlement by the Ohio Company, formed by a number of wealthy Virginia planters and prospectors, including, among others, Augustine and Lawrence Washington.

Under the authority of the British crown, the Ohio Company laid claim to some 500,000 acres, and British interests in the region were defended by a number of fortifications, which they had negotiated with Native Americans for permission to build. The French, however, also had soldiers in the area, and between the French and the British there was a sort of first come, first served race to build fortifications and claim territory before the other could do so. At the Forks of the Ohio, between the Allegheny and Monongahela Rivers, lay the British forts. The French began extending their presence in the Louisiana territory northwards an effort to build an unbroken line of defenses that would cut the British off from further expansion of their territory, which sparked outrage amongst the British royal authorities in Virginia.

A Royal Envoy

"The many and repeated complaints I have received of these acts of hostility lay me under the necessity of sending, in the name of the King, my master, the bearer hereof, George Washington, Esq., one of the Adjutants-General of the forces of this dominion, to complain to you of the encroachments thus made, and of the injuries done to the subjects of Great Britain, in violation of the law of nations, and the treaties now subsisting between the two Crowns."

Extract, Letter from Governor Dinwiddie to the French Commander in the Ohio Country, 1753

The royal governor of Virginia, Robert Dinwiddie, was, like the elder Washington brothers, a shareholder in the Ohio Company, and thus he had a considerable financial stake in preserving British claims in the area, in addition to his duty to uphold the expansion of the crown's colonial authority. But in 1753, though open hostilities with the French seemed certain to erupt soon, the conflict had yet to escalate beyond the reach of diplomatic courtesies. Governor Dinwiddie was instructed by the crown to send an official British envoy to the French with a message demanding that they abandon their expansion into the Ohio Country, on pain of an armed response by the British. When Washington got wind of the fact that Dinwiddie had received this message, he immediately petitioned Dinwiddie to make him the envoy who would convey it to the French. Despite the fact that he was only 21 years old, Dinwiddie agreed to his request, both on the basis of Washington's close family connection to the Ohio Company, and Washington's experience traversing the frontier (a difficult and dangerous task which probably few others were eager or able to undertake).

Washington's journey west, begun in November of 1753, was arduous even by the standards of the frontier travel he had undertaken before.

Washington and his companions reached the Forks of the Ohio safely by December, where they entered into negotiations with the Seneca tribe of Native Americans, in an effort to gain intelligence about French movements and secure an escort to Fort La Boeuf, where the French commander resided. The chief of the Seneca was named Tanacharison, also called the Half King, and he favored the British over the French because he was under the mistaken impression that the British only wished to trade in the region and had no interest in settling in the Ohio Valley. Washington did not correct him, and while his diplomatic overtures to Tanacharison were more or less successful, the escort Tanacharison provided Washington was much smaller than he had hoped for.

In December, after making contact with one French commander and being redirected to his superior officer, Washington delivered the message he had been entrusted with to a Captain de Saint-Pierre, who received him politely, but did not acknowledge any intention of complying with the demand to vacate the territory seen by the British as belonging to them. Washington made careful note of the arrangements of the French defenses and returned to Williamsburg to report back to Dinwiddie. There, at Dinwiddie's request, he wrote a monograph in a single day, entitled *The Journal of Major George Washington*, which Dinwiddie had published. It gave a thrilling account of Washington's perilous journey into the Ohio Country, as well as his interactions with the French commanders. Such frontier narratives were a wildly popular genre of literature in the eighteenth century, and Washington's was widely read. Not only did his account stir up national feeling in Britain against the French threat in the Ohio Valley—it made George Washington, for the first time in his already remarkable life, quite famous.

In the following excerpt of the *Journal,* which displays Washington's abilities as an author of clear and engaging prose, he describes the attempts of the French to win the loyalties of Tanacharison and his men over from the British:

"The Commandant ordered a plentiful Store of Liquor, Provision, &c. to be put on Board our Canoe, and appeared to be extremely complaisant, though he was exerting every Artifice that he could invent to set our own Indians at Variance with us, to prevent their going 'til after our Departure : Presents, Rewards, and every Thing that could be suggested by him or his Officers. —I can't say that ever in my Life I suffer'd so much Anxiety as I did in this Affair ; I saw that every Stratagem that the most fruitful Brain could invent, was practised, to win the Half-King to their Interest, and that leaving Him here was giving them the Opportunity they aimed at."

Now a celebrity both in Britain and in the American colonies, Washington was somewhat dismayed by the meagerness of the financial reward he received for his endeavors on the frontier—a mere 50 pounds, which barely covered his expenses. But within a week of his return to Williamsburg, he would have something infinitely more valuable to him than either money or fame: a promotion.

Lieutenant-Colonel Washington

As district adjutant of the Northern Neck of Virginia, Dinwiddie commissioned Washington to raise a militia and return with it to the Ohio Country. Construction of a British fort at the Forks of the Ohio had begun in Washington's absence under the supervision of a man named William Trent, and Washington's men were to assist in its completion.

Washington was disheartened by the men he was set in command over. Militias, especially in the colonies, were not like professional armies; the men who served in them were completely untrained. They were poor, illiterate, often the dregs of society, and received so little support from the colonial government that they were not outfitted with uniforms or weapons, but expected to fight in whatever rags they possessed, with whatever weapons they could scrounge. Washington wrote to the governor asking for better pay and more support, but his requests were refused. The regiment which he led into the Ohio Country in April of 1774 numbered 160 men.

Governor Dinwiddie's orders to Washington regarding the terms on which he was to engage the French militarily were phrased in a way that left them somewhat open to interpretation. He was ordered to take only defensive actions, but at the same time to imprison, kill, and destroy any French soldiers who threatened British interests. Crucially, Dinwiddie had not received these orders from England; his instructions to Washington were issued entirely on his own authority. And while Britain was not officially at war with France, Dinwiddie's orders were virtually guaranteed to provoke an open conflict almost as soon as Washington arrived in the region.

Before Washington reached the Forks of the Ohio, news came by courier that the French had taken the fort that was being constructed, overwhelming the 34 British soldiers with a force of 1000 troops. This being a rather more uneven confrontation than any of the militiamen had bargained for, they threatened to desert, as did Tanacharison, who was assisting Washington once more. To assuage Tanacharison, Washington told that a great number of British troops were only a short distance away. To assuage his militia, Washington wrote to the royal governors of Pennsylvania and Maryland asking that they send troops; this was a rather extraordinary thing for him to do on his own authority, but the governors of both states must have been favorably impressed by his stirring rhetoric, because they agreed to his request.

Governor Dinwiddie, on the other hand, was less amenable to providing Washington's men with necessities. Colonial soldiers, including both common recruits and officers, were paid considerably less than regular British troops and officers with royal commissions. Washington was so insulted by his low pay that he declared to Dinwiddie that he would rather serve his country as an unpaid volunteer than accept a salary that valued him so much less than a commissioned officer. But he begged for better pay for his troops, declaring that he could scarcely see why men in their position would bother to fight when they could dig a ditch for a similar wage. Dinwiddie was irritated by these complaints, and considered them unreasonable. This would not be the last time that Washington was set in charge of poorly trained militias who did not receive adequate pay from the government; these same issues would plague the Continental army when Washington took command some twenty years later.

Massacre at Jumonville Glen

While Washington's troops moved through the dense wilderness foliage, they received word from Tanacharison that a large encampment of French lay nearby. Furthermore, Washington reported to Dinwiddie that they had for many days heard rustling noises in the woods around them, which made Washington deeply suspicious that the French were spying on them in preparation for a surprise attack. Washington and his men spent days in a state of elevated anxiety, jumping at noises in the dark, moving silently in the dark and the rain to avoid an ambush.

On the advice of Tanacharison, Washington decided to mount a preemptive attack against the French troops, which, he felt, were essentially stalking his men and biding their time before launching their own assault. Early in the morning on May 28, 1754, Washington's men surrounded a small encampment of thirty five

Frenchmen who were entirely unaware of their approach. What happened next has been a source of debate for centuries, as Washington's report and the reports of the surviving French soldiers contradict one another. According to Washington's account, his men were spotted by one of the French soldiers, and the French began to fire on them. (The French, perhaps not surprisingly, maintained that Washington's men fired first.) But the French had been unprepared, and were actually having breakfast when the fight began; their causalities amounted to over half of their men, while only one man was killed on the British side, and two wounded.

The French officer in charge was an officer and nobleman by the name of de Jumonville, and he identified himself to Washington, declaring that he had a diplomatic message from the French government demanding the withdrawal of British soldiers from the region; it was, essentially, the same message Washington had delivered to the French only a few months before. Washington's version of events stated that after Jumonville was taken prisoner, he began reading the diplomatic message aloud, until, half way through it, Tanacharison came up behind him and split his head in two with a hatchet. The French, on the other hand, claimed that a British soldier shot Jumonville on Washington's orders.

Either way, this was a shocking and potentially disastrous turn of events. The official French position was that Jumonville had been a diplomatic ambassador, and therefore untouchable under the rules of civilized war. Washington, who maintained all his life that Jumonville was not killed by his orders, nonetheless felt that a genuine ambassador would have approached him directly, as Washington had done when delivering his message to the French.

Washington wrote an account of the matter to Dinwiddie in Virginia and instructed his men to build a makeshift fortification on the spot where the skirmish had taken place, which he named Fort Necessity. He knew the French would retaliate, and indeed a counter-attack by a large French force under the command of no less a person than Jumonville's own older brother came on July 3, 1754. Washington's men were routed, and he was obliged to sign a surrender. The articles of capitulation were written in French in a crabbed hand, and it was translated for Washington in the middle of the night, in the rain; as a result, Washington ended up signing a confession that stated that he had willfully assassinated Jumonville, or had him assassinated by his order. Washington was deeply dismayed when he discovered his mistake, and fiercely denied that he had ordered an assassination, but the fact that his signature appeared on the articles made him infamous in France and a figure of notoriety in Britain, where only months before he had been a celebrated figure.

The Battle of Monongahela

Fortunately for Washington, his reputation recovered in only a short time. In Virginia, the story of his defeat at Fort Necessity began to be seen more in the light of a valiant military stand to the last man than a disgraceful series of blunders. In 1755, Major General Edward Braddock came to Virginia at the head of two regular British regiments with orders to re-take Fort Duquesne from the French. (Fort Duquesne was the fort at the Forks of the Ohio which Washington and his men had been on his way to help build in April of 1754.) He promptly invited Washington to join his staff, but Washington had resigned his commission in October of 1754 in protest against the fact that colonial officers were required to take orders from British officers even if they were of a lower rank. He instead volunteered to serve Braddock as a civilian aide de camp, which would oblige him to take orders from no one but Braddock himself, but which would once again have him outfitting a military expedition at his own expense.

Braddock treated Washington courteously and valued his extensive knowledge of the frontier, but he proved stubborn in one important point. From his disastrous encounters with the French, Washington had learned that the best way to wage a battle while ensconced in the hills, rivers, and forests of the American frontier was to emulate the expert example of the Native Americans, who used the cover of trees and foliage to sneak up on their enemies and vanish back into cover before they could strike back. The French, Washington told Braddock, had fought as the Indians fought, while Washington, at Fort Necessity, had met the attack in the traditional European style, which was to blame for his overwhelming defeat. Braddock, however, was not interested in the military advice of a mere colonial who lacked the professional training of a real British soldier. In his opinion, the sneak attacks of the Indians couldn't possibly make the least impression on a regiment of trained British soldiers. He intended to make war in the same style in which Europeans had been making war for centuries: shoulder to shoulder, in tight formation, as if marching out to face the enemy on an open plain.

To provide context for non-historians, England, in the eighteenth century, was the most powerful nation in Europe, and the British army was seen, in both England and America, as invincible. The arrival of Braddock's forces would put a quick and decisive end to French incursions into the Ohio territory, it was believed. On this basis, Washington may well have thought that matters would work out for the best even if Braddock didn't take his advice about frontier fighting styles.

Another point which sometimes eludes Americans studying the early history of their country is that Americans in the first half of the eighteenth century saw themselves, unequivocally, as English, and thus heirs to all the privileges that being English could bestow. Washington, certainly, was proud of being Virginian, but his pride was related to the belief that as a wealthy and pre-eminent Virginia landowner, he was the equal of any young English lord of similar stature. What his military career was teaching him was that, in the eyes of the mother country, a colonial—even a white man with plenty of land and money—would always be second best. This realization dismayed and confounded Washington, particularly when this English condescension resulted in his own expert advice on frontier warfare being neglected.

The consequences of Braddock's superiority were disastrous. His regiments, amounting to some three thousand men, were encumbered by wagons full of heavy supplies, despite the fact that Washington had warned Braddock that the regiments would need to travel lightly over the hilly terrain. Men and horses died in the attempt to push and haul the grain wagons up hillsides. And the pace of the regiment train was so slow that it advanced only 2 miles a day. On Washington's advice, Braddock agreed to send about half the men ahead at a much faster pace.

On July 3, 1755, Indians allied with the French attacked the British regiments in almost the precise manner Washington had attempted to put Braddock on his guard about. With loud ringing "war-whoops", such as the British soldiers had never heard before, Native American fighters fired from behind the cover of trees, and just as quickly disappeared, before the British could so much as aim at them. The rapidity of the attack, the strangeness of the Indian war cries, and the seeming impossibility of defending themselves, sent the professional British soldiers into a panic. As Washington would write later to Dinwiddie, "the Virginians behaved like men and died like soldiers [while the] dastardly behavior of the English soldiers exposed all those who were inclined to do their duty to almost certain death."

Braddock's aides and officers were scattered; losses were so heavy that the remaining soldiers did not know where to look for orders. During the long trek from Virginia, Washington had come down with dysentery; in fact, he had it to such a severe degree that for several days the doctor had forbidden him to ride on horseback and had instead made him lie down in the back of a wagon. He was profoundly ill and exhausted, having received multiple applications of the finest medical treatment the eighteenth century could offer for his illness: bleeding. But when the Indian attack came, Washington sprang onto horseback and joined the fight; when his horse was shot from beneath him, he took up another. Because of his height of 6 feet or more, Washington made a prominent target in battle, and four bullets passed through his coat and hat, but he was not wounded. Braddock, however, took a bullet to the lung. Washington personally carried Braddock to safety, and then, after a day-long battle and a night of no sleep compounding the ravages of his illness, Washington rode 40 miles to convey Braddock's orders to one of the other divisions.

The British defeat at the Battle of Monongahela was an intensely harrowing experience for Washington, but his unswerving attention to duty, his physical courage, and his energy throughout the battle had drawn the attention of every person, British or Indian, who survived to report about it. When Washington returned to Virginia in late July of 1755, he found that his reputation as a fearless war hero was fixed before the public.

Colonel Washington of the Virginia Regiment

Washington's exhausting 40 mile ride to convey General Braddock's orders to the commander of the rear division had put Colonel Dunbar on high alert. Refusing either to advance to the scene of the battle or hold his ground, Dunbar ordered a retreat to Fort Cumberland, and eventually withdrew with his men to Philadelphia. Emboldened by their unexpected victory at the Battle of Monongahela and by the absence of the British forces, Indians carried out devastating raids on British settlers all along the western frontier.

Governor Dinwiddie's response was to reform the disbanded Virginia Regiment and place Washington at the head of it under the rank of colonel. His job, and that of the regiment, was to defend the Virginia frontier against the raids of the French and Indians. His job was made the more difficult by the same problems which had plagued his command during his last stint in the Virginia Regiment, that is, the quality of the men who joined his militia. In the first place, few persons wished to join, as the pay was meager and the danger was great. Washington's recruiting officers were accused of forcing recruits to join under threat of being locked up without food, or even killed. Washington disciplined his recruiting officers for this sort of behavior, though it wasn't far off the standard for militias at the time. Desertion rates were again high, and it isn't difficult to see why; most people had only joined the militia under duress in the first place, and precious little glory would they get out of it. Only professional soldiers, enlisted of their own free will, trained for a suitable period of time, properly outfitted by the government, and paid a decent salary, could be relied upon to accomplish the feats of military discipline that Washington dreamed of. Washington conceived a profound distaste for militias from this period, though later, when the Revolutionary War broke out, he would find that even a badly trained militia could fight heroically, given the proper motivation.

British forces in North America had been placed under the command of the Earl of Loudon. Washington took time away from the Virginia frontier to visit Lord Loudon in Boston, who frustrated Washington with further proof that colonial regiments would never attract notice for the same deeds of bravery that would have heaped honors on a regular regiment of British soldiers. Lord Loudon, though favorably impressed by Washington personally, cared little at all for goings-on in Virginia. Washington returned to the Virginia frontier to find that the region had been devastated by raids, sending a steady stream of settlers fleeing back east in fear for their lives. Washington's letters of this period demonstrate extraordinary frustration and depth of feeling over his inability to protect those settler families who were relying on him; but colonial military matters were confused under Lord Loudon, and the help Washington requested was not forthcoming. Washington became known for his fierce military discipline during this period, and while his disciplinary measures were in keeping with the standard practices of the British army in the eighteenth century, they were nonetheless horrific: floggings of up to 1500 lashes were not uncommon, and all repeat deserters were hanged in public from a 40 foot high gibbet.

While Washington encountered tremendous frustrations during his tenure as the appointed guardian of British settlers in the western Virginia frontier, those settlers who lived in the 350 mile region for which he was responsible suffered fewer losses from raids than any of the other frontier territories during this period.

Chapter Three: Master of Mount Vernon 1759-1775

Martha Dandridge Custis

Washington had become infected with dysentery during the Braddock campaign, and he suffered a severe recurrence of the disease in 1757. In typical stoic fashion, he attempted to ignore the fact that he was ill until he was so weak that he couldn't walk. He was forced to leave his duties as commander of the Virginia Regiment and return home for an extended period of recuperation. He developed a cough during his convalescence, and became fearful that he was coming down with tuberculosis, the disease which had killed his brother Lawrence. But a visit to a doctor confirmed that he was only recovering from the dysentery and that there was no infection in his lungs. Relieved, Washington turned his attention to domestic matters.

Under the terms of Lawrence Washington's will, George was to inherit Mount Vernon in the event that Lawrence's wife Ann and daughter Sarah died without heirs. Ann Fairfax Washington remarried 6 months after Lawrence's death, and not long afterwards Sarah Washington died at the age of four. Washington was now the heir, rather than the heir presumptive, to his family's most picturesque property. After Ann's relocation to her new husband's estate, prior to Washington's taking command of the Virginia Regiment, he rented Mount Vernon from his sister in law and took over management of its farms. When illness forced him to take a step back from his military career, Washington began renovating the Mount Vernon farmhouse in the style of an English country manor. He was becoming reacquainted with the charms of a planter's life just as his view of military service as a colonial officer was souring. As Washington, now about 27, settled into life on his estate, his thoughts began to turn to marriage.

It was shortly after receiving the news that he was free of tuberculosis that Washington first made the acquaintance of the woman who was to become his wife. Martha Dandridge Custis was an extraordinarily wealthy young widow with two children. She was about 8 months older than Washington, and renowned for the sweetness of her temper. While not much is known about George and Martha's courtship, it must have been rapid. The timing of events suggests that Washington made a visit to Martha's home shortly after learning that she had been widowed; her youth, wealth, and the colonial custom of swift remarriage made her highly attractive and eligible, and Washington was well aware that he was not the only suitor she would receive.

In 1758, Washington made two visits to Martha's home—which was known, somewhat amusingly to modern readers, as White House—before returning to the command of the Virginia Regiment for the last time. Both George and

Martha's correspondence suggests that he probably proposed to on his second visit, because they both sent orders to their English clothing merchants for wedding clothes immediately afterwards.

What must George Washington have been like to marry? Physically, Washington was reckoned to be handsome: he was six feet tall and immensely strong and hardy, an impression which was no doubt reinforced by his famous reputation as a war hero. The fact that he survived so many grueling expeditions into the wild American frontier attests to his health and personal vigor—bouts of malaria, smallpox, and dysentery notwithstanding. He was reported to have quite large hands, and a head that appeared slightly too small in relation to his frame, as well as broad hips and large thighs, which supposedly contributed to his skill on horseback.

As to his personality, one of Washington's leading characteristics was his extraordinary reserve and stoicism. Historian Ron Chernow attributes Washington's remarkable self-control partly to his relationship with his mother, who criticized him constantly and rarely praised him, and partly to his enormous ambition. Conscious of the limitations of the social class into which he had been born, Washington was determined to rise above his station. A European education, such as his brothers Lawrence and Augustine had received, would have helped him imitate the manners of his social superiors. Denied such an education, Washington bridged the gap between the unpolished manners of his own upbringing and the social graces of the wealthy by a rigorous course of imitation and self-improvement on a scale that brings to mind *The Great Gatsby* (though without the tragic outcome). Aware that he had a prodigious temper and a passionate nature that might lead him to say or do impetuous things in the presence of those he wished to impress, Washington compensated by keeping himself under rigid control. But the passionate nature was still there, informing his actions. In his early twenties, Washington wrote love poems about the girls he was courting, or attempting to court. In marriage, his affection for his wife was obvious to everyone who observed them together, and Martha was known to be the one person who could make him laugh at himself.

Obviously, Martha didn't know that she was going to be the wife of the first president of a brand new country, but if she had known, she could scarcely have been more qualified for the job of the nation's first First Lady (though in fact, the title of First Lady wasn't used until after Martha Washington's time.) Martha Dandridge was born to a family not unlike Washington's: middle class gentry who owned some land and a few slaves. She was an enthusiastic reader of novels and newspapers, though she was not especially well educated, and her letters demonstrated little regard for spelling, punctuation, or grammar. The slaves her family owned mostly worked in the fields rather than in the house, so Martha was trained to manage a household, which in the eighteenth century was not unlike being apprenticed to a skilled trade. She would have learned how to produce her own thread and cloth, in addition to sewing all the clothes her family needed. Animal husbandry, vegetable gardening, cooking, and the production of household remedies would all have been a part of her training.

Daniel Custis, Martha's first husband, was the son of one of the wealthiest men in Virginia. Martha was 18 when they met, and Daniel was 38; legend has it that they met in church. There was some opposition to the marriage from Daniel's father. Daniel had never married before, which was highly unusual for a man of his age, but this was due largely due to the fact that his father wished him to marry a woman with a fortune of her own, and had stood in the way of several attempted courtships. Martha, by contrast, had only a small dowry, but her personal qualities seem to have won her prospective father in law over, and he gave his blessing for the match shortly before his death.

In marrying Daniel Custis, Martha achieved an enormous and unexpected social boost, not unlike those which characterized Washington's career. Rather than working to provide for her household, Martha was now the mistress of 12 household slaves who did the work of the house under her direction. She was converted from a working farm girl into a high society hostess almost overnight. One can speculate that Martha and George found that they had a great deal in common when they began comparing personal histories; both would have been able to relate to rapid, dizzying elevations of social status, and the challenges that came with such elevations for those who had been accustomed to simpler lives.

Martha and Daniel Custis had four children, two of whom died before they were five years old. The surviving children, Jack and Patsy, became Washington's step-children. Daniel Custis died after he and Martha had been married for only 7 years, and he died without leaving a will; this meant that, rather than the management of his estate being transferred to a male relative, Martha was legally responsible for all of it. Though it would not have been uncommon for a widow in Martha's position to hire or even request the assistance of a male manager, she chose to undertake the settlement of Custis's estate and management of his properties herself. Considering that the estate was comprised of some 17,000 acres and the labor of 300 slaves, the fact that she managed to oversee that season's harvest was in itself quite remarkable, let alone all the other extra duties that had fallen on her. Managing a plantation of such a size was more than a full time job in itself, however, and so was managing a household. While Martha had no financial need to remarry, the idea of sharing such enormous burdens with another rational adult must have been highly appealing.

Final Expedition of the Virginia Regiment

One last, brief military interlude occurred in Washington's life before the long period of marriage and domestic bliss he would enjoy prior to the American Revolution. In April of 1758, a few weeks after his second visit to Martha Custis at White House, Washington learned that the British were sending a fresh supply of 7000 troops to the Ohio Country for one last attempt at taking Fort Duquesne back from the French. They were under the command of a Brigadier General John Forbes, who, despite his contemptuous feelings regarding colonial officers in general, rated Washington's abilities pretty highly, particularly owing to Washington's frontier expertise.

Washington was now 27, and with marriage before him, he was beginning to turn his attention to local politics. Everyone who was anyone in Virginia society had held a seat in the House of Burgesses, including Lawrence Washington and William Fairfax, Washington's most important influences. He had been defeated in a last minute bid for election a year prior, but in 1758 he was elected to the seat for Frederick County, Virginia, with an overwhelming majority of the votes. Washington was immensely popular in his home state, not only due to his grand reputation as a soldier, but because of a conflict that arose with Forbes at the outset of his last Ohio campaign. Forbes had to choose between two roads when plotting out the route to Fort Duquesne, one of which passed through Pennsylvania. The other, Braddock's Road, passed through Virginia and had been forged by Washington himself; it was the site of Braddock's disastrous defeat and death at the Battle of Monongahela. The colony whose road was chosen would reap significant economic boosts, and accordingly, Washington lobbied Forbes extensively—one might even say excessively—for Braddock's Road. Though Forbes ultimately chose the Pennsylvania road (and became rather annoyed with Washington for his interference in the matter), Washington's campaign on behalf of Virginia's interests made him a hero back home.

The Forbes campaign was distinguished by two events significant to Washington's career. The first was a tragic friendly fire incident between two groups of soldiers from the Virginia regiments. Upon hearing a bout of gunfire from ahead of the line, Washington determined that soldiers from the regiment had been ambushed from the forest, just as had happened to Braddock's men the previous year. Forbes allowed Washington to ride to their aid, but the soldiers under attack mistook the sounds of Washington's men coming to relieve them for an advance by French or Indian troops; the two groups of Virginians fired on each other before Washington could stop them, and more than thirty men were killed or wounded. The incident made such an impact on Washington that he remembered it to the end of his days.

The second was the capture of Fort Duquesne, which, though a triumph for the British, came as something of a let-down after so many years of fighting. The Indian scouts once loyal to the French had abandoned them after spying the advance of nearly 2500 British soldiers. Thus deserted, the French commander ordered a retreat from the fort, leaving behind only a skeleton crew of soldiers, who set fire to it once the British came in sight. The victorious British troops rebuilt the structure, naming it Fort Pitt, after the British prime minister.

The seizure of Fort Duquesne meant that Washington had finally helped to secure a greater measure of safety for the British settler families in the Virginia frontier who had once looked to him for protection. With his marriage forthcoming, it seemed an auspicious moment for retirement and a change of energies from the martial to the domestic. Washington's officers evinced genuine grief at his departure; he had a talent even then for winning respect and loyalty from those who served under him.

Marriage and Domestic Life

George Washington married Martha Dandridge Custis on January 6, 1759, at Martha's home, White House. This alliance, though it provided ably for Washington's happiness in most respects, also laid a great deal of responsibility on his shoulders. Washington was wealthier on paper than in practice; most of his assets were tied up in land and slaves. Martha Washington had only inherited one third of her husband's estate; the other two thirds were set aside for her children's inheritance, and, as Washington became the children's legal guardian, he was legally accountable for managing their property until they came of age, without being free to do with it as he wished. He was "land rich but cash poor", and as a result, most of his spending was done on credit.

It is strange to think that the difficulties Washington encountered in furnishing Mount Vernon should have had any role in provoking the American Revolution, but in a way, the two things were directly related. Anything that a rich colonial wished to purchase in the way of finery had to be imported from Europe because the colonies did not have the means of manufacturing it. For Washington and the other wealthy planters of Virginia who sought to emulate the lifestyles of English gentlemen, this meant that fine cloth, such as silk and velvet, and all the notions and fripperies that adorned their clothing—lace, buckles, tassels, etc—had to be ordered from English tailors. (The fact that Washington had to order so much of his clothing from abroad is responsible for the fact that we know so much about his physical dimensions; in order for his clothes to fit, he had to send very precise measurements. Washington is often remembered as being 6'2 or 6'3, but we know this is incorrect because he told his tailors that he was about 6 feet tall.)

But it wasn't only clothing that had to be imported. The wood of the native trees of Virginia were not considered distinguished enough for elegant furniture, so when Washington wanted a mahogany bed frame, that too had to be ordered from England. Likewise, the fine china tea services, silver and ivory utensils, and crystal drinking glasses of Washington's stores were all of European make. Farming instruments such as plows had to be ordered from abroad as well. And if anything arrived in less than sterling condition, Washington either had to make do or order an immediate replacement—it would take the better part of a year to send a plow back to England for a refund, which was longer than he could afford to wait before harvesting his crops.

The difficulty with this arrangement lay in the fact that Washington, and all wealthy Virginians dependent on trade with Britain, perceived their London agents as being inclined to take advantage of their colonial customers. Because their American customers lived so far away, it was, naturally, easier for English merchants to fob off poor quality goods on them than on domestic customers who could examine items before purchase, or return them easily. And the English merchants knew they had the Americans over a barrel. By law, American colonists were required to do all their trading with Britain—that was rather the point of having a colony, from the English perspective. Finally, American planters like Washington were actually dependent on their English agents for all the money they made from their harvests—American colonists weren't going to buy all, or even most, of Washington's enormous tobacco crop, and a planter could scarcely be both at home overseeing his farms and in England selling his crops at the same time. The same agents who handled Washington's orders for china, linens, and velvet breeches were responsible for selling Washington's tobacco overseas—and not necessarily at the best price possible, if they were inclined to be lazy, because no matter how well or poorly it sold, they were able to pay themselves first before returning the remainder to Washington.

Washington's suspicion of English traders fed into the same vein of resentment he had been cherishing against the British since he first came up against the brick wall of British condescension towards all things colonial. Once again, it is crucial to remember that the American colonists, particularly wealthy and important ones like Washington, saw themselves as being on the same social level as persons of the same social class in England. That is to say, they saw themselves as English, an important distinction in a world which quaked in fear of the British empire. The realization that the British themselves did not see it that way—that in fact, they esteemed American colonists just as meanly as colonists from such distant holdings as, say, the Caribbean—came as a harsh blow to Washington's pride. His London agents would not dare to play such tricks with him, he believed, if they did not feel entitled to look down upon all colonials.

Many historians have noted that if Washington had been given the kind of respect and preferment in the militias that a young English officer of similar ability and courage would undoubtedly have received, the American Revolution might have had a very different outcome than it did.

The Stamp Act of 1764

"And for and upon every pack of playing cards, and all dice, which shall be sold or used within the said colonies and plantations, the several stamp duties following (that is to say):

1.   For every pack of such cards, *one shilling*.

2.   And for every pair of such dice, *ten shillings.*"

Excerpt, Stamp Act, 1763

One of the most famously remembered slogans of the American Revolution is "no taxation without representation." The Stamp Act was the beginning of the series of draconian taxation policies imposed on the colonies by the English Parliament to recoup Britain's losses from the French and Indian War that the slogan referred to.

As a soldier in the Virginia militia, Washington had already encountered the English attitude that the colonial soldiers, far from being entitled to the same pay as English soldiers, should rather be grateful that they were being paid at all, since it was their own land and people they were defending. Washington had no patience for such rhetoric; Virginia and the other colonies were "the king's dominions", his men the king's loyal subjects, deserving the same pay and honors as any British soldier.

But the notion that the American colonies had been the beneficiaries of a very expensive war which tripled Britain's debt was the prevailing one in Parliament, and thus it was decided that Britain's losses should be repaid out of American pockets. The Stamp Act of 1764 required an official seal, not unlike a modern passport stamp, to be affixed to a certain class of paper documents, including legal documents, almanacs, and playing cards. To get the stamp you had to pay, which was how the tax was collected.

The real bone of contention for colonial political leaders wasn't necessarily that the tax was ruinously unaffordable, or even the injustice of being made to pay for the recent war. It lay in the fact that never before had Americans been taxed by the British crown directly. The power of levying taxes in the colonies had always rested with the House of Burgesses. It was, in fact, illegal under British law for taxes to be imposed on people who were not proportionally represented in the parliamentary body that taxed them. Parliament's levying taxes against the American colonies in this manner was not merely extortionate and unjust, it effectively denied that American colonists had the same rights and privileges as English subjects.

The Stamp Act was met with such inflammatory oppositional rhetoric in the Virginia House of Burgesses (the rhetoric was mostly delivered by Patrick Henry, of "give me liberty or give me death" fame) that the royal governor dissolved the house and called for new elections. Washington looked with dismay on the violent protests that were breaking out over the new taxes, but he was as disgusted by them as anyone.

The Stamp Act was eventually repealed, but it was followed in short order by the Declaratory Act, which stated unequivocally that Parliament could tax the colonists any time it liked (making a tax which had been technically illegal, legal), and the Townshend Acts, which placed a tax on items such as paper, glass, lead, paint, and tea. Washington and a number of other wealthy Virginians responded with a somewhat ingenious measure that not only placed significant financial pressure on the British to repeal the Acts, but enabled Washington and others like him to solve the problem posed by their lack of available cash: they instituted a boycott against all British goods covered by the Townshend Acts. Washington's enthusiasm for this plan was inspired equally by his growing rage against the British and his desire to reduce his significant personal debt to his British agents. He reasoned that it was nearly impossible to stop spending in the manner he had become accustomed to without appearing to reduce his standing in the eyes of his neighbors— but with the boycott as his excuse, he could practice greater frugality and no one would think to question it. Since many of his neighbors were in exactly the same predicament with their own creditors, the boycott proved a popular measure amongst all the Virginia planters.

With the dissolution of the House of Burgesses, the society which was formed to enact the boycott became the de facto decision-making body in colonial Virginia. (It named, among its members, one of the newly elected burgesses, a young man of 26 who scarcely had a chance to enact the duties of his office before it was terminated by the governor: Thomas Jefferson.)

The boycott against the Townshend Acts was successful, to a certain extent. In a move that was calculated to take the wind out of the sails of the colonial opposition while nonetheless asserting Parliament's continuing absolute authority to impose whatever taxes it liked, all of the Acts were repealed—except, famously, for the one that imposed the tax on tea.

If we were making a study of the Revolutionary era in general rather than the life of George Washington in particular, this would be the point at which we began to examine a period of deepening unrest in Boston. Boston was the site of many of the revolution's most iconic events, as the Boston Massacre, in which British soldiers fired into a crowd of people protesting the Townshend Acts, and the Boston Tea Party, in which a group of revolutionaries calling themselves the Sons of Liberty threw overboard 90,000 pounds of tea owned by the East India Company.

These events had thundering repercussions across all thirteen colonies, and Washington's first steps towards revolution were taken in direct response to the fact that Boston swiftly ended up in the crosshairs of an infuriated British empire. But life in Virginia remained fairly peaceful during the late 1760's and early 1770's—a period of increasing political tensions at the highest levels of society and government, but little in the way of outward violence or conflict. Washington would soon be drawn into the fulcrum of the revolution, but he had to travel to get there.

Jack and Patsy Custis

The pre-Revolutionary years at Mount Vernon saw Martha Washington's son and daughter grow from small children to adolescents and young adults. Because Martha had lost her two eldest children when they were very small, she was a doting and somewhat anxious mother, blind to her children's faults and hypersensitive to the state of their health. In the case of Patsy, her sensitivity was unfortunately justified; Patsy began suffering from the effects of severe epilepsy when she was twelve, which made it impossible for Martha to feel easy about leaving her side for a single moment, owing to the accidents that could befall her during a fit. George Washington's correspondence demonstrates an enormous affection for his step-daughter, as well as a touching desire to make up for the poor health she suffered by lavishing her with expensive presents.

Patsy's older brother Jack was no less beloved by his mother, but Washington's feelings towards him were somewhat different. Jack had no earthly cares and nothing but the inheritance of a vast estate to look forward to when he reached adulthood; as a consequence, neither Washington nor any of Jack's teachers could persuade him to do any serious work or apply himself to any serious endeavor. When Jack was 19, Washington sent him to college in New York, but he had already become engaged to a girl of 16, and he only remained at college for a short time before he left, impatient to be married. Washington was distressed by the suddenness of the match, convinced that Jack should not marry until he was older. Nonetheless, he and Martha quickly became very fond of Jack's fiancée, Nelly Calvert.

Nelly was at Mount Vernon visiting her in-laws to be in June of 1773 when Patsy Custis died after a last sudden seizure. Her death was quick and apparently painless, but Martha and George were both devastated. Strange though it sounds, Patsy's dying when she did had a profound effect on the future of the American Revolution; the third of the Custis estate that was being held in trust for her passed to Jack and to her mother, and the sudden windfall of cash enabled Washington to clear his debts with his London agents.

This easing of financial pressure meant that when war broke out, Washington was free to leave the management of Mount Vernon in the hands of deputies and take command of the Continental army. Patsy's death, like that of Washington's father, his brother Lawrence, his sister in law Ann, and his niece Sarah, deprived Washington of a family member he dearly loved, yet benefited him enormously in a financial sense.

The Fairfax Resolves

In 1774, in response to the Boston Tea Party, the British imposed punitive measures on the city of Boston in an attempt to force its people into paying back the cost of the tea that had been destroyed—about a million dollars in today's money. Known as the Coercive Acts in Britain, and the Intolerable Acts in the America, they provoked extraordinary outrage throughout the colonies, even in the south, normally somewhat removed from goings-on in the north of the country.

The Coercive Acts ordered the closure of Boston's port, which crippled the city economically, and revoked Massachusetts's right to self-rule by bringing all colonial government posts under the authority of the royal governor. They also stated that any British soldier or government official who was accused of a serious crime would have to be tried in England, where colonial witnesses could not easily travel to testify against them. The last of them, the Quartering Act, required colonists to provide lodging for British soldiers. The law regarding the trials of British soldiers was particularly galling, as the soldiers who had fired on the American crowd during the Boston Massacre had been acquitted of most charges after being ably defended by John Adams, then a lawyer in the city.

The lasting effect of the Coercive Acts was rather the opposite of the one they were intended to achieve; the colonies, perhaps for the first time, began to conceive that what affected one colony affected all. The individual colonies were politically and culturally distinct from one another, and the unity of the whole had barely been contemplated. But Washington had begun to sense the necessity of a strong central government for all the colonies while he was in the Virginia regiment, and when the Coercive Acts struck Boston, he began to perceive that the plight of Boston would soon be the plight of all of America. To express solidarity with Massachusetts, Washington and other Virginians banded together to send money, flour, and wheat to the poor of Boston, who would be most affected by the closure of the port. They also declared a day of fasting and prayer.

Because the House of Burgesses had been dissolved, Washington and his fellow elected officials had taken to meeting in a private room in a pub in Fairfax County to discuss political matters. They had resolved to invite delegates from across the colony to a Virginia Convention (which would serve as a blueprint for the better-known Constitutional Convention in about a year's time.) With his neighbor, George Mason, Washington drew up a list of resolutions intended to clarify Virginia's stance regarding its own rights, as they perceived them, and also regarding actions that should be adopted in the future.

The first of these resolutions provides a fascinating insight into the mindset of these wealthy, privileged Virginians who seemed to feel the slights of their imperial masters more keenly, in some ways, even than the poorer colonists who suffered more immediately from British strictures. It has been reproduced below.

"Resolved, that this Colony and Dominion of Virginia cannot be considered as a conquered country, and, if it was, that the present inhabitants are the descendants, not of the conquered, but of the conquerors. That the same was not settled at the national expense of England, but at the private expense of the adventurers, our ancestors, by solemn compact with, and under the auspices and protection of, the British Crown, upon which we are, in every respect, as dependent as the people of Great Britain, and in the same manner subject to all his Majesty's just, legal, and constitutional prerogatives; that our ancestors, when they left their native land, and settled in America, brought with them, even if the same had not been confirmed by Charters, the civil Constitution and form of Government of the country they came from, and were by the laws of nature and Nations entitled to all its privileges, immunities, and advantages, which have descended to us, their posterity, and ought of right to be as fully enjoyed as if we had still continued within the Realm of England."

The turn of phrase employed in the first sentence in particular is extremely revealing. These aristocrats from Virginia were not rejecting an imperial, colonial system as an evil, though the American Revolution is sometimes construed in those terms; the evil lay in the fact that Americans, or at least these Americans, believed they had a right to be treated with the same dignity as their own colonial masters. Plantation masters like Washington presided at the head of what were, in effect, small self-reliant villages; they were accustomed to unquestioned power. The king had reminded them once too often that under the present system, all that power could be taken from them in the blink of an eye. It was a rude awakening for many.

Almost equally interesting is the fact that one of the Fairfax Resolutions called for an end to importing any more slaves to Virginia. This was not the same thing as abolishing slavery by any means, nor was it necessarily as liberal-minded as it sounds; in the 1760s, Washington had diversified his crops, abandoning tobacco for wheat and corn. These crops were far less labor intensive than tobacco, and as a result, amongst the slaves of Mount Vernon there were now an abundance of field hands with nothing to do.

In essence, Washington had too many slaves on his hands—more than it was profitable to support, now that he didn't need their labor. But he was conscientiously opposed to selling slaves if he could help it. Washington answered this financial quandary by having his slaves retrained as craftsmen and artisans, but other slave owners were in similar predicaments. Since Virginian planters could count on the slave population increasing through natural population growth, there was little financial viability in importing any more to the colony. However, there is something in the manner of the resolution's phrasing that implies a moral dimension to Washington's thinking on the subject:

"Resolved, that it is the opinion of this meeting, that during our present difficulties and distress, no slaves ought to be imported into any of the British Colonies on this Continent; and we take this opportunity of declaring our most earnest wishes to see an entire stop forever put to such a wicked, cruel, and unnatural trade."

Note that it is not the institution of slavery which is "wicked, cruel, and unnatural", but the slave trade. The nuance is important. The kidnapping, transportation, and selling of African people at auction were aspects of slavery rarely witnessed by most of those who profited from slave labor. The sight of a newly imported slave being sold on the auction block was shocking in a way that the sight of a field hand or house servant in relatively good health laboring for their master's benefit was not. The visceral horror of slavery was much more difficult to ignore or justify when it couldn't be dressed up in euphemistic terms, such as when Washington referred to his domestic staff as his "family".

In the final reckoning, authoring the Fairfax Resolves transformed Washington from an interested bystander in the events leading up to the revolution to an active participant. The fame he had won during the French and Indian War was rekindled as his co-authorship of the Resolves became known.

First Continental Congress

The Fairfax Resolves were presented to the Virginia Convention, where they were swiftly adopted and put into action. More importantly, following the convention, Washington was elected as one of the seven Virginia delegates sent to the First Continental Congress in Philadelphia, from September to October of 1774, where he would, for the first time, meet figures crucial to the future of the republic, such as John Adams.

Nobody who attended the First Continental Congress was thinking of permanent separation from England yet. The delegates still believed (or chose to maintain the fiction) that the king could be persuaded to see reason and would eventually overrule his unreasonable ministers and come to America's defense against Parliament's unjust taxes and military retributions. However, there were so many soldiers in Boston that the possibility of an armed conflict in the near future was on everyone's minds.

Washington was by far the most famous soldier in colonial America, and no other North American officer had commanded a larger number of soldiers. He was aware that Congress might need to raise an army in the future, and that his name was being mentioned in private conversations about who ought to lead it. This suited Washington, but he deliberately did not put himself forward, aware that the last person the delegates were likely to set in a position of power over them was someone who appeared too eager for such power. Military high commanders, everyone was exquisitely aware, were uniquely placed to become dictators, and dictators, obviously, were just what the colonists were trying to avoid. Washington had the sensitivity to perceive this, and made a point of appearing modest, retiring, and sensible—the soundest political strategy he could have employed.

Back home in Virginia, the colonists were already raising militias. Many of them wanted the famous soldier George Washington to be their commander, and he became the flag officer of four different volunteer troops in 1775. The royal governor of Virginia had no desire for his own colony to become the site the first armed conflicts of the American resistance, and he attempted to pressure Washington into giving up command of the militias by hitting him where it hurt the most—in Washington's inexhaustible appetite for acquiring land. The governor threatened, on a flimsy legal pretext, to revoke Washington's title to more 17,000 acres which had been awarded to him for his service in the French and Indian War. But it was too late. The cause of American independence did not yet exist, but Washington was already inexorably committed to the cause of resisting British tyranny.

Chapter Four: General Washington of the Continental Army 1775-1777

Lexington and Concord

There is no single, universally agreed upon starting point for the American Revolution. The American colonies were declared by Parliament to be in a state of rebellion in February 1775, which authorized the escalated deployment of British soldiers to the colonies. Some consider the first casualty of the war to be Crispus Attucks, who was either an escaped slave or a free man of color, and was the first person to be killed in the Boston Massacre in 1770. But the most popular start date for the war is April 19, 1775—the date of the Battles of Lexington and Concord, and the so-called "midnight ride of Paul Revere" immortalized by the Longfellow poem:

He said to his friend, "If the British march
By land or sea from the town to-night,

Hang a lantern aloft in the belfry arch
Of the North Church tower as a signal light—
One if by land, and two if by sea;
And I on the opposite shore will be,
Ready to ride and spread the alarm
Through every Middlesex village and farm,
For the country folk to be up and to arm."

The reference in the poem to "the British march[ing] by land or sea" had to do with the attempted capture of two ringleaders of the American rebellion in Boston, John Hancock and Samuel Adams, who were hiding in Lexington. British General Gage had orders to arrest them, and to march afterwards to the town of Concord, to capture a supply of gunpowder.

The Americans had excellent intelligence of British troop movements in the area, and were able to warn Hancock and Adams in time for them to evade capture. In Lexington, 700 British Regulars were met by 77 colonial militiamen; shots were fired, and 8 colonists were killed.

Afterwards, the British marched to Concord; after four hours of searching for the powder, they discovered that the colonists—now calling themselves Patriots—had moved all their munitions and supplies to a new hiding place.

As the British marched back to Boston, rebel Minutemen (militia members who practiced maneuvers in order to be ready to fight at a minute's notice) were waiting to ambush the British from the cover of the trees on either side of the road. Two hundred and thirty British soldiers were killed by the Minutemen, and 90 colonists were killed by the British. In the eyes of many, this was the point of no return, after which no amount of diplomacy could restore a peaceful relationship with Britain.

Second Continental Congress

It was not until the Second Continental Congress, which convened in May of 1775, about a month after the battles of Lexington and

Concord, that some delegates began calling for a final, official severing of ties between America and Britain. Most delegates were still unprepared for such an extreme measure; however, even those not yet ready to declare complete independence from Britain recognized that the conflict had become violent, and that the colonies would need to be prepared to defend themselves against the British soldiers who had been sent to the colonies to enforce the king's decrees. George Washington was so alert to the martial spirit of the times that he turned up to the Congress dressed in his old uniform from the French and Indian War.

While all the colonies were up in arms against Britain in the metaphorical sense, only the northern colonies were armed in the literal sense. Congress proposed to reinforce the northern militias with soldiers from Pennsylvania, Maryland, and Virginia, but the combining of militias from different colonies required the appointment of a commander to oversee them and shape them into a single fighting unit. As Virginia was the colony with the largest population, and as the southerners were fearful that a northern commander in charge of northern troops might attack the south after he had bested the British, a Virginian commander was necessary. Of the several men who were considered for the role, three hailed from that colony; but Washington's command experience outstripped theirs by far.

But the fact that Washington was the most experienced military commander in the American colonies didn't mean much in comparison to the skill and training of British commanders in charge of British soldiers. When Washington was offered the command of the Continental army on June 15, 1775, he accepted it with a short speech in which he emphasized his own awareness that he was under-prepared for the task he'd been given:

"Though I am truly sensible of the high honor done me in this appointment, yet I feel great distress from a consciousness that my abilities and military experience may not be equal to the extensive and important trust. However, as the congress desire it, I will enter upon the momentous duty and exert every power I possess in their service and for the support of the glorious cause...But lest some unlucky event should happen...I beg it may be remembered by every Gentleman in the room that I this day declare, with the utmost sincerity, I do not think myself equal to the command I am honoured with."

It is difficult to doubt Washington's sincerity, given that he repeated so many variations on this sentiment in the days and weeks following his appointment, not only in public but in his private correspondence. But there is an implicit contradiction between his words, which were self-effacing, and his actions, which were clearly the actions of a man who desired the post he had been offered. He was too intelligent and politically canny not to understand that he was being considered for the position, and that his modest aversion to openly campaigning for command was the tactic best calculated to win it.

The conflict between ambition and self-awareness seemed to create an uncomfortable tension in Washington. On the one hand, he was accustomed to putting himself forward for military commands when chance placed them in his way, as was evident from his campaigning for commissions during the French and Indian War. On the other, he seemed aware that, even if he was in a better position than any other American to lead the war, he was being appointed to a nearly impossible task—and if he failed at it, his reputation would be sunk in ignominy forever, no matter how many disclaimers he had issued. To accept the command was to accept responsibility for the outcome. It was almost as if he couldn't help himself; ambition, perhaps, required him to get hold of the command and make the best of it, but he couldn't help quailing at the thought of all the ways it might go wrong.

But duty must also have been his motivation, and it is rarely easy to disentangle duty from ambition in the careers of great military leaders. As we mentioned earlier, Washington was the only American who had ever commanded a force comprised of troops from multiple colonies. He was also more familiar than anyone else with the British army's proven inability to adjust its fighting methods to the terrain of North America. No one knew Britain's military weaknesses as intimately as Washington, who at one time had studied them from the perspective of a loyal subject who hoped for nothing more than a royal commission. As a patriotic American, he could not avoid the responsibility of command, but the very qualifications that made him best suited to the role meant that he knew better than anyone else how low the odds of success were.

The First Year of the War

Washington's appointment as commander of the Continental army was met with cheering crowds in the streets and a dispatch warning him that British General Howe had routed a rebel position in the Battle of Bunker Hill. Though a defeat in the technical sense for the Americans, the battle had come as an enormous shock to the British, who suffered about a thousand casualties—far more than expected from a fight with untrained, disorganized colonials. The severe blow which the battle dealt to the British lent a sheen of optimism to Washington's first months in command—an optimism that would prove unfortunately misplaced, as the Continental army was in tatters even before the war got truly underway.

Washington encountered the same problems in the Continental army that he had bemoaned as the commander of the Virginia Regiment. The militias were comprised of volunteers serving on short term contracts, while the British Regulars were professional soldiers, the best provisioned and most highly trained army in the world. Washington wanted soldiers who were clean, orderly, disciplined, sober, and ready to take orders; instead, he had tavern keepers and farmhands who defecated in the camps because they couldn't be bothered to walk all the way to the latrines, argued with orders because they'd elected their own officers, and were drunk as often as they could manage it. Washington was given to observe, somewhat mournfully, that no sooner had the officers managed to teach their men how to fight than their contracts were up, and the officers had to start again with a fresh batch of recruits.

From 1775 to 1776, some of Washington's most important decisions as commander in chief of the Continental army had surprisingly little to do with troop movements or military intelligence. For instance, he considered smallpox (quite correctly) to be a more deadly enemy than anything wearing a red coat. He knew how debilitating smallpox was, having survived a mild bout of it in 1751 in Barbados (and he considered his having contracted it then as a providential occurrence, as it rendered him immune to the very disease most likely to ravage his encampments.) Washington took strict measures to fight the spread of disease amongst his army. He consigned any of his men who came down with smallpox to strict quarantine until after they had recovered. Somewhat more daringly, by 1776 he was requiring every man in the Continental army to receive a smallpox inoculation. In the late eighteenth century, inoculation was still a brand new medical procedure; it had only been performed for the first time in England in 1722. The procedure was not widely practiced in colonial America, as doctors were scarce, and their patients feared that the procedure would only make them sick. The inoculation of Washington's soldiers saved the army from losing massive numbers to disease.

Washington's other unconventional military strategy involved lying to everyone—including the Continental Congress—about the fact that the army possessed only enough powder for each soldier to shoot off about 9 rounds. He had been told on taking command that the army possessed around 300 barrels of powder, only to discover that the actual number was closer to 40. Washington knew that if word of the powder shortage got back to the British, they would not hesitate to attack in force, confident that the rebels would quickly run out of ammunition. Telling anyone, including the civilian leaders of the revolution, could risk an intelligence leak.

As a result of this, Washington was forced to appear more reticent than he wished in ordering attacks against the British, as he could not afford to waste powder on anything other than a fight with excellent odds and a near guaranteed win. This frustrated Congress, who could not understand the reason for Washington's hesitation. But Washington refused to defend himself; there were too many delegates to be certain that all of them would keep it secret. The fact that Washington was able to keep the powder shortage a secret was a remarkable achievement, and constituted one of his most extraordinary feats as commander of the army.

Washington's principle accomplishment during the first year of the war involved driving the British forces under General Howe out of Boston. After seizing Fort Ticonderoga from the British in upstate New York, Henry Knox transported their canons to Dorchester Heights, an elevated site overlooking Boston. The transformation of Dorchester Heights from undefended ground into a fortress took place overnight, under cover of darkness, and it startled Howe so badly that his forces retreated the next morning.

The victory in Boston was an important one for the Continental army, but prospects for the immediate future darkened when Washington received word that George III, who in addition to being the British monarch was also the Prince of Hanover (one of the states which is now part of Germany), had hired 17,000 Hessian mercenaries to fight on his behalf in the New World. Superiority of numbers was the one thing the Americans had on their side; such a number of Hessians, who were well trained and well armed, made the British threat considerably more deadly.

The Declaration of Independence

"We hold these truths to be self-evident, that all men are created equal, that they are endowed by their Creator with certain unalienable Rights, that among these are Life, Liberty and the pursuit of Happiness.--That to secure these rights, Governments are instituted among Men, deriving their just powers from the consent of the governed, --That whenever any Form of Government becomes destructive of these ends, it is the Right of the People to alter or to abolish it, and to institute new Government, laying its foundation on such principles and organizing its powers in such form, as to them shall seem most likely to effect their Safety and Happiness."

Excerpt, Declaration of Independence, July 4, 1776

Despite the amount of American blood that had been shed in the conflict with Britain thus far, there were still those who hoped for an ultimate reconciliation with the king as late as the summer of 1776. Washington considered any hope of reconciliation to be delusional, and with some justification. It was with relief and gratification that he greeted the Continental Congress's formal Declaration of Independence, a copy of which made it into his hands on July 6, 1776, courtesy of John Hancock.

Guessing correctly that it would rouse his men to high spirits, Washington dispatched copies of the

Declaration to each brigade of his troops, and ordered it read aloud. American soldiers in New York celebrated by tearing down and beheading a lead statue of George III at Bowling Green, then melting the lead down for ammunition.

The Declaration of Independence represented a point of no return for all who had signed it, and for every man who was known to be a leader of the rebellion: they had made themselves officially traitors, pitted in a treasonous conflict against the British empire. Anyone who was caught would undoubtedly be hanged. Washington was so sensible of the fact that the British would wish to make an example of him that he took time to plan a scheme for avoiding capture. He also decided how he would answer the charges if he were captured and tried (in other words, that he would plead guilty and not attempt to defend himself from treason charges.)

The Battle of Brooklyn and the New York Campaign

Washington's victory in Boston was followed by a resounding defeat in New York that very nearly brought a disastrous early ending to the war for the American army.

With Boston secured, Washington's army moved to defend the city of New York against the British navy. Washington knew that there was little or no chance that he would be able to hold the city. The many rivers and inlets leading from New York's harbor made it an ideal battleground for the British fleet under Howe. While the British army was formidable, it was the British navy that outmatched every other military force in Europe; their ships were fast, and their movements difficult to track. The closest thing that Washington had to an American navy were the merchant ships that had converted themselves into privateers, state-sanctioned pirate vessels that captured enemy ships, took one third of their supplies, and turned the rest over to the Continental army. American privateers could not effectively repel the British naval presence in New York, however, and the abundance of waterways meant that there were an abundance of opportunities for the British to creep into the city by stealth.

Washington was aware that Howe was settling troops on Staten Island, presumably in a run up to an attack on the American position, but days passed with no movement. Washington couldn't understand why the attack was delayed for so long, when Howe was obviously preparing to make a move of some kind. Two critical errors set Washington up for defeat when the attack finally did come. First, Washington had received reports that the British had about 9,000 men, when in fact they had 22,000. Second, the British made a three-pronged attacked against Brooklyn by approaching from the west, toward the center of Brooklyn, and from east Brooklyn near Jamaica Pass. The first two points had been anticipated by Washington, but the third had been left mysteriously unguarded. The British were able to flank the Continental army and surround it in preparation for a siege.

Such a siege would inevitably have been short-lived; the Americans would have been forced to capitulate, the army been taken prisoner, and the war would have been over, if not for the fact that Washington followed this humiliating defeat with a brilliant tactical maneuver. Under cover of heavy fog and a dark, rainy day, Washington ordered a stealth retreat from Brooklyn across the East River to Manhattan. Nine thousand American soldiers disappeared under Howe's eye overnight.

The New York campaign in the winter of 1776-1777 was full of harsh lessons for Washington and disasters for the American army. It was a period of intense distress and mental strain for the general; he felt let down by his officers, betrayed by his generals, and dismayed by his ragged, constantly shrinking army. There were other setbacks and inglorious defeats during this period, such as the loss of Fort Washington under the command of Nathaniel Green. But this first winter of the war gave rise to some of Washington's most iconic moments as a commander, and Washington's failures in New York inspired the far more successful strategy the American army would pursue in the future: luring the British into the countryside, away from the support of their ships, and using the rugged terrain to their advantage.

The Delaware Crossing and the Battle of Trenton

As a commander, Washington's finest moments were dramatic, daring, and stealthy. The arming of Dorchester Heights and the retreat from Brooklyn both demonstrated his capacity for creativity in the fact of impossible challenges and his preference for bold action whenever possible. But if there is a single moment in the course of the Revolution for which Washington is more famous than any other, it is probably the 1776

Christmas Delaware River crossing, immortalized in the painting by Emmanuel Leutzer. This action was planned along the same daring and secretive lines as Washington's remarkable feats in Boston and Brooklyn, and amounted to one of Washington's greatest successes during the war.

Washington's army had, in the end, not only been pushed out of Brooklyn, but out of New York entirely; many American soldiers had been captured by the British in Manhattan, and British General Cornwallis had chased the army across the whole of New Jersey. By December of 1776, the Continental army had retreated from New Jersey into Pennsylvania for the winter, while the British forces under Howe remained encamped in New York, and the Hessian mercenaries who were fighting for the British were encamped in New Jersey, near Trenton.

It was traditional in European warfare in the eighteenth century for winter to be a period of limited hostilities, as the ice and snow posed a greater danger to the men, horses, and provisions of both sides than open battle did. In fact, winter was generally such a peaceful period that Martha Washington made the yearly journey from Virginia to join her husband at his winter camps. But it was not a period of truce; an attack in winter was less likely to be attempted because of the extra dangers involved, but a skilled maneuver was all the more likely to be successful for the same reason.

Washington, furthermore, was under a kind of deadline; most of his troops were militia, and their period of enlisted service was over on New Years' Day, after which the majority of them would simply melt away, back to their homes and farms—or they might take advantage of Howe's recent offer to pardon any rebel who swore an oath of loyalty to the king. After the many disasters of the New York and New Jersey campaign, Washington did not hold out much hope that enough new recruits would join the army to make up their losses. He felt strongly that if he did not make some decisive move before year's end, the army would dissolve before it could be defeated.

Washington decided, therefore, to launch a surprise attack against the Hessian mercenaries in the early hours of the morning on the day after Christmas; the American commanders planning the action believed the Hessians were likely to have been celebrating the holiday and drinking long into the night. (In fact, while the Americans did find the Hessians groggy and unprepared, this was due to the increased vigilance of night time patrols, and not to drunkenness.)

Washington's men crossed at four separate points along the river, which made the operation dangerously complex, but increased the chances that at least one of the companies would reach the Hessians, even if the others were slowed down by Cornwallis's men, who were stationed at outposts along the New Jersey border.

Cornwallis's outposts were not the greatest danger to the Continental army, however. There was so much ice upon the Delaware River that, in places, Washington's men had to lean out over the ends of the boats and break it up a little at a time. Elsewhere, dangerously large and sharp chunks of ice floated downriver, and had to be evaded by the skilled fishermen amongst Washington's troops. Sleet and heavy winds made the crossing even more dangerous, especially since most of the American soldiers could not swim, but the noise and the lack of visibility ensured that the Hessians would not see them coming.

Washington's men did not reach the Hessian camp until 8 a.m., and not all of the groups that attempted the crossing were able to make it across. But the surprise attack that followed, later called the Battle of Trenton, was a success: around 900 Hessian mercenaries were taken prisoner, with others dead and wounded, while American casualties were in the single digits.

Washington's men also seized Hessian arms and provisions, which they desperately needed. Because not all of his men had made the crossing, Washington did not attempt to hold the city of Trenton and canceled his plans to attack the cities of Princeton and New Brunswick. His military strategy from now on would involve quick attacks, followed by strategic retreats, rather than European style pitched battles or the siege and defense of cities.

Washington returned to Pennsylvania with his Hessian prisoners in tow. His victory at Trenton proved to be a vital turning point in the war. While not especially important from a tactical point of view, the fact that the American army, even in a pitiable and ragged state, were able to defeat a large force of professional European soldiers, proved an incalculable psychological boost both to the army itself and to America as a whole. Congress renewed its financial support, and troop enlistments after the New Year redoubled.

Washington's Family

"What a date, My Dear Heart, and what a country from which to write in the month of January! It is in a camp in the middle of woods; it is fifteen hundred leagues from you that I find myself buried in midwinter. Not too long ago, we were separated from the enemy by a small river; now we are seven leagues away from them and it is here that the American army will spend the winter in small barracks hardly more cheerful than a jail. I do not know if the general ... will decide to visit our new abode; should he, we would show him around. The bearer of this letter will describe to you the pleasant place which I seem to prefer to being with you, with all my friends and amidst all possible pleasures."

Extract, letter from the Marquis de la Fayette to his wife, 1778

Since this book is meant to be a study of the life and character of George Washington, and not merely an examination of Washington's actions during the Revolution, we should pause briefly for a look at Washington's personal relationships during the first years of the war. Washington's frustrations with the quality of the men who fought in the militias meant that he was continually on the lookout for young officers who could make up some of the deficit in training. He preferred to advance the careers of young men of his own social class—men from genteel families, who owned property—because he believed they were likely to possess superior educations, and to care more than another person about how their actions in the war would reflect on their reputations.

As the war dragged on, however, Washington became somewhat more inclined to merit ability, intelligence, and loyalty even in those who were not especially well born. Washington gathered these talented and able young officers around him; they acted as his aides de camp, and the most trusted commanders in his army. In his correspondence from this period, Washington referred to these people as his "family".

Perhaps the most important member of Washington's wartime family was the one who would enjoy the least fame in the decades after the war. His name was Billy Lee, and he was one of Washington's slaves. Lee, about 18 years Washington's junior, had been purchased by Washington along with his brother Frank when they were boys. Both brothers were assigned as house slaves at Mount Vernon; Billy worked as Washington's valet, and Frank served as the Washingtons' butler. Lee was a superbly talented horseman, and he served as Washington's master of hounds during fox hunts, which were Washington's favorite leisure activity. During the war, Lee was by Washington's side every second, which is extraordinary when you consider that Washington made a point of being in the thick of the worst danger during every battle he was present for. After the Revolution, many men who had seen far less danger and spent far less time in Washington's company became famous and built life-long reputations on the back of their war records, but Lee was rarely mentioned. He appears in at least one portrait of Washington that was painted from life. Billy Lee was the only one of Washington's slaves who was freed and given a pension on Washington's wills—the rest of his slaves were not freed until the death of Martha Washington.

Speaking of Martha Washington: in consideration of the fact that she spend about half the war in Washington's camps and worked to assist him during these times, she is reckoned by some historians as having performed the duties of an aide de camp, and accordingly as deserving to be recognized for her contributions to the war. At least one historian has noted that the most important role which Washington's aides played was that of a confidante to whom he could air his frustrations. They were, in this way, substitutes for his wife when his wife was not available. Considering how invaluable confidantes were to Washington's ability to withstand the pressures of command, Martha's presence in the camps no doubt made a considerable difference to morale.

Other notable persons who won Washington's esteem and trust in the first year of the war included Nathanael Greene, Henry Knox, and Alexander Hamilton.

Nathanael Greene was a Quaker and major-general of the Rhode Island militia whom Washington met after taking command of troops in Boston. His physical daring and courage made him one of Washington's most trusted commanders, a trust which backfired somewhat when Washington left to Greene the decision of whether or not to defend Fort Washington or abandon it before a British assault. Greene chose to defend the fort, against Washington's advice, and the fort was lost, along with a great many valuable provisions. Nonetheless, Washington chose to give Greene another chance to prove himself, and he went on to drive Cornwallis out of North and South Carolina during the southern campaign of 1780.

Henry Knox was a book shop owner and amateur engineer who also first became known to Washington during the siege of Boston. Together with his wife Lucy, he helped Washington to forge social connections with his guests; Washington was miserably bad at small talk, while the Knoxes were sociable and gregarious. Knox was instrumental to the American victory at Boston, having helped to capture Fort Ticonderoga and its canons, which formed the chief armaments at Dorchester Heights. He became the new nation's first Secretary of War after the Revolution.

Alexander Hamilton was undoubtedly the most famous of Washington's wartime protégés. Born in the West Indies, Hamilton had made the journey to America in order to attend college. When he first came to Washington's notice, Hamilton was an artillery captain whose bravery during the New York campaign stood out in stark contrast to the behavior of many other officers and the mass desertions of the enlisted men. Hamilton was initially reluctant to accept a position directly under Washington, being eager for opportunities to earn battlefield promotions, but eventually he became Washington's chief of staff. Hamilton's mother was French, and he spoke French fluently; this was a tremendous boon to Washington, who had never learned the language, but received a great deal of correspondence from French officers who came to America in search of commissions. Hamilton resigned from Washington's service on a pretext as the war drew nearer its end, until Washington at last agreed to give him a command, shortly before the Battle of Yorktown. After the war, when Washington became president, Alexander Hamilton was appointed the nation's first Secretary of the Treasury.

The young aide to whom Washington was closest, on an emotional as well as a professional level, was the legendary Marquis de Lafayette. Only nineteen years old when he first came to America, Lafayette's military experience was limited, though not non-existent; he was commissioned an officer in the Musketeers when he was fourteen, and he had read books on warfare, not unlike Washington as a young man some twenty years earlier.

France was the historical enemy of England, and in eighteenth century Europe wars were considered a quick way to earn fame and wealth—for these reasons, it had become commonplace in the early years of the revolution for professional French officers to appear in America and "offer" their services, in exchange for a large salary, a high rank, and a large command. Lafayette, however, was extremely wealthy, and like Washington, offered to fight for no pay at all. Lafayette had inherited a number of aristocratic titles when he was two years old, after his father was killed in a battle with the English; he was left orphaned and extremely wealthy at the age of 11, when his mother died.

Historians are united in agreeing that Lafayette looked up to Washington almost as a father, and that Washington returned his affection. Lafayette was so romantically passionate about the American cause that he had sailed to South Carolina on a ship loaded with donations of food and supplies in defiance of a royal order. He was not given a command until Washington was satisfied that he had learned all he needed to know about battlefield military strategy, but during the time he served as Washington's aide, he exhibited the greatest fervor for his work, and above all, gave Washington the gift of his unswerving personal loyalty.

Chapter Five: Washington On the Brink 1777-1781

The Conway Cabal

The revolution was an immensely fragile time for American identity. The average patriotic colonist did not switch from calling themselves British to calling themselves American as soon as the Declaration of Independence was signed. They were more likely to call themselves Virginians, Marylanders, New Yorkers, etc. The colonies knew that they wished to be free of British control, but there was not yet any consensus that they were, or would ever be, one unified nation. "The United States of America" did not exist; and as a consequence, the people who were fighting for their freedom had little in common. For much of the war, nothing really united them except for their belief in George Washington.

Washington was more than just the commander of the American army: in the eyes of the world, he *was* America. At a time when the country had no anthem, no flag, and not even a unanimously agreed upon name, Washington was the face of the movement. The virtues for which he was famous—strength, audacious courage, aristocratic nobility—were, in the foreign press, transferred to the cause he represented. The rebellion of the American colonies had come as an enormous shock to the royal courts of Europe. Rebellions were scarcely unheard of, but no royal colony had ever launched a rebellion this well organized, under the guidance of such gifted personalities. And while, from the American perspective, their defeats seemed to outnumber their victories, the fact that an army of poorly provisioned rebel volunteers had achieved any victories whatsoever against an army of Britain's caliber seemed scarcely short of miraculous. Rightly or wrongly, Washington was given most if not all of the credit for this by foreign observers.

Despite his popularity amongst the American people, however, Washington was anything but universally popular at the uppermost levels of Congress and the military. Many leaders of the rebellion were of the opinion that Washington's virtues were grossly exaggerated out of the sheer need for the people to put their faith in someone. Others were fearful of the extraordinary power Washington wielded, and looked for ways to lessen the scope of his influence, lest he should be tempted to turn into a dictator. Others of Washington's detractors were mere petty rivals for power.

One of this latter group was Thomas Conway, an Irish born soldier who served in the French army before coming to America. He sat at the center of a loosely organized group of men who were quietly advocating for the command of the army to be transferred to General Horatio Gates. Evidence of this exists in the form of a number of grumbling letters which they wrote to one another behind Washington's back.

The motivation for this half-hearted attempted coup was Washington's defeat at the Battle of Brandywine Creek, which coincided with a spectacular and unexpected victory for Gates at the Battle of Saratoga, in which British General John Burgoyne and his entire army were taken prisoner. The victory at Saratoga was enormously important to the outcome of the war. News of Burgoyne's defeat and capture finally tipped the hand of the French king, who chose to officially declare support for the United States by making two treaties with emissary Benjamin Franklin. The recognition of American sovereignty by a major foreign power did more to legitimize the American cause in the eyes of the rest of the world than two Saratoga victories. According to reports, Washington was so powerfully affected by the news that France had become an official ally of his struggling young country that he burst into tears, while Lafayette kissed him on both cheeks.

Despite the embarrassment of Washington's defeat at Brandywine Creek, and other embarrassments such as the British occupation of Philadelphia, the Conway Cabal fizzled to an end after having had little effect, save to increase Washington's stress level for a short period of time. Washington was not without his faults as a commander—he preferred to spend a long time deliberating his choices before making up his mind, which gave him a reputation for being indecisive—but he was aware of his weaknesses, and was always eager to receive criticism that would help him to correct his faults. He found it hurtful when he was criticized behind his back, however; disloyalty of that nature was abhorrent to him. The Conway Cabal lost traction after at least two letters making reference to it found their way into Washington's hands.

Furthermore, Lafayette played an important role in silencing Washington's critics in Congress, by reminding them that Washington embodied America, as far as the French were concerned. If Washington were forced out of power, he intimated, the French would very likely lose interest in their alliance.

Winter Encampment at Valley Forge

After Washington's crossing the Delaware, the image of him that Americans are probably most familiar with is Washington at Valley Forge, the Pennsylvania field where Washington's army made camp for the winter during each year of the war, starting on December 19, 1777. While historian Ron Chernow is insistent that the famous painting depicting Washington kneeling in the snow and praying for his troops is allegorical rather than drawn from life (Washington would never have done anything so ostentatious as pray outdoors where his men could see him) the snow on the ground is decidedly non-metaphorical.

The conditions under which American soldiers passed the winter of 1777-1778 at Valley Forge are legendarily harsh, but for once, the legend does not exaggerate the reality. Clothing was so scarce that many men had no shirts, let alone coats to shield them from the cold and snow. Washington famously observed the bloody footprints in the snow, left by the more than two thirds of the soldiers who had no shoes. They had no blankets to sleep under, which made it difficult to get rest. Food was scarce or nonexistent; diseases such as typhus, dysentery, smallpox, and pneumonia ran rampant, and many men lost body parts to frostbite. The makeshift hospital near the camp had no medical supplies to treat the ill and wounded. Washington and his aides slept on the floor of a single two story house tended by a single fire. It has been estimated that at least 2000 soldiers died of disease and exposure at Valley Forge that winter. Indeed, obtaining adequate provisions for the army was such an ongoing problem throughout the war that many more Americans died of illness and poor living conditions than were killed by the British.

The privations endured by Washington's men during this period seems to have altered his feelings about the army he had been placed in command of. In 1775, he had seen little that impressed him; he had lamented over the mass desertions and general lack of military discipline, convinced that such men scarcely qualified as soldiers. But after the winter of 1777, he seemed unable to praise American soldiers in sufficiently generous terms. To American General George Clinton, Washington wrote a letter criticizing Congress for providing adequate funds or supplies to the army. In describing their suffering, he said that anyone hoping for American victory in war must pay greater attention to these matters:

"I mean the present dreadful situation of the army for want of provisions, and the miserable prospects before us, with respect to futurity. It is more alarming than you will probably conceive, for, to form a just idea, it were necessary to be on the spot. For some days past, there has been little less, than a famine in camp. A part of the army has been a week, without any kind of flesh, and the rest for three or four days. Naked and starving as they are, we cannot enough admire the incomparable patience and fidelity of the soldiery, that they have not been ere this excited by their sufferings, to a general mutiny or dispersion."

Washington continued to visit harsh punishments on deserters, but he had lost his amazement that so many attempted to desert; on the contrary, he seemed amazed that any of them remained of their own free will.

Conditions at Valley Forge began to improve somewhat towards the spring of 1778. Blaming a large part of the army's misfortunes on improper handling of supply lines, Washington assigned one of his most trusted commanders, Nathanael Greene, as the new quartermaster general. In February of that year, two important arrivals at the camp lifted the spirits of the American army and transformed a quiet battle of endurance into a spirited preparation for a resumption of hostilities against the English in the summer. The first arrival was that of Martha Washington, who took it upon herself to tend to the soldiers' needs as best she could, making shirts, darning socks, and traveling all around the camp to visit the sick and injured and make note of where the worst needs lay.

The second February arrival to the camp was the self-styled Baron Friedrich von Steuben. A Prussian officer during an era when Prussian armies practiced more advanced methods of military discipline than anywhere else in the world, Steuben began a ruthless training program in Washington's winter encampment that would transform the ragtag collection of farmer and innkeepers into true professional soldiers. He did not speak English, and no one in the American camp spoke German, but he was able to communicate with French-speaking officers such as Alexander Hamilton, and to his personal aide, who translated his orders.

Steuben drilled the American soldiers relentlessly. He ordered the camp reorganized along hygienic principles to prevent disease (for instance, he insisted on the use of latrines). Under Steuben's instruction, the American army learned to march in formation, to load and unload their weapons with brisk efficiency, and to use their bayonets for something other than spit-roasting their food. The training methods Steuben devised at Valley Forge were collected as a booklet which was used in the U.S. army until the Civil War.

Battle of Monmouth

One of Washington's greatest critics during the war was a fellow Virginian and former friend, General Charles Lee, a former officer in both the British and Polish armies who had been personally disappointed not to have been offered the command of the Continental army over Washington. Washington had a high opinion of Lee's abilities at the beginning of the war and had urged Congress to give him a command. Lee had blundered his way into getting captured by the British some sixteen months earlier, after leaving the protection of his army to spend the night with a woman at a nearby inn; British soldiers, eager to take an American general prisoner, had surrounded the house and marched Lee away dressed in only his night shirt. Lee was treated well during his captivity, as the British were hopeful that he could be persuaded to defect.

In the mean time, the British forces in America had undergone a change of command. General Howe had resigned, and General Henry Clinton, who replaced him, began withdrawing his army from Pennsylvania to New York. They were encumbered by a bulky supply train, which slowed their progress, and Washington devised a plan to strike at the lumbering British baggage train in New Jersey. A number of Washington's generals, including Charles Lee, opposed this plan, but Steuben, Lafayette, and Hamilton were all strongly in favor of it.

Washington initially offered command of the attack at Monmouth to Lee, who refused it. But when Washington decided to place Lafayette in charge instead, Lee changed his mind. This proved a near-disaster; when Lee found that the soldiers at the back of the British column were prepared for the attack, he became confused and called for an almost immediate retreat, without sending word of his actions back to Washington. This was particularly distressing to Washington, because the Battle of Monmouth was one of the rare occasions during the war when American forces actually outnumbered the British; by the odds alone, the battle should have been a resounding American victory. This was also the first chance Washington's army had been given to demonstrate the fighting skills that Steuben had taught them in the winter and spring at Valley Forge.

Washington was incensed by Lee's retreat, and lost his temper in a monumentally public fashion, calling Lee a "damned poltroon". Washington mounted a horse and took command of the retreating troops personally in a pitched battle which lasted the rest of the day in weather so hot that many men, and Washington's own horse, dropped dead of heat stroke. Eventually the British retreated. Washington's men made camp on the battlefield, ready to start the fighting again first thing in the morning, but when he awoke, he discovered that the British had sneaked off towards New York in the middle of the night. After the battle, Lee attempted to defend his actions, but he was convicted by a court martial and suspended from military service. Washington declared the Battle of Monmouth a victory for the Americans. It was the last major battle fought under his command in the north until nearly the end of the war three years later.

The Treachery of Benedict Arnold

"In the firm persuasion, therefore, that the private judgment of an individual citizen of this country is as free from all conventional restraints, since as before the insidious offers of France, I preferred those from Great Britain; thinking it infinitely wiser and safer to cast my confidence upon her justice and generosity, than to trust a monarchy too feeble to establish your independency, so perilous to her distant dominions; the enemy of the Protestant faith, and fraudulently avowing an affection for the liberties of mankind, while she holds her native sons in vassalage and chains.

I affect no disguise, and therefore frankly declare, that in these principles I had determined to retain my arms and command for an opportunity to surrender them to Great Britain;

and in concerting the measures for a purpose, in my opinion, as grateful as it would have been beneficial to my country; I was only solicitous to accomplish an event of decisive importance, and to prevent as much as possible, in the execution of it, the effusion of blood."

Excerpt, "To The Inhabitants of America", by Benedict Arnold

One of the first major American victories in the war was the capture of Fort Ticonderoga in 1775. General Horatio Gates received the credit for that feat, but it was perhaps equally the doing of General Benedict Arnold. Unlike persons such as Gates and Lee, Arnold never clashed personally with Washington, and Washington was entirely unaware that Arnold was nursing any grievances. However, Arnold had been passed over for promotion by Congress, despite having nearly lost his leg during his early wartime heroics. Arnold was also instrumental in the capture Burgoyne and his entire army in 1776. He was one of Washington's favorite generals, and Washington trusted and relied on him implicitly.

By 1780, the theater of the American Revolution had grown complex. Washington had been forced to spend most of 1779 attending to the political and diplomatic aspects of his job. The actual fighting had moved south to Charleston, from which position British General Banastre Tarleton was waging a bloody war against the Americans in North and South Carolina and Virginia. Around the same time, the French began to send aid to the American cause in the form of a small flotilla of ships and an expeditionary force of soldiers, under the command of the Comte de Rochambeau. With the appearance of the French ships, the British no longer had uncontested naval supremacy in American waters. Washington's immediate thought was of driving the British out of New York; the northern city had become the principle stronghold of the British forces in America, ever since Washington had been driven out during the campaigns of 1775. Washington had been attempting to come up with a plan to retake the city ever since, and he believed the French ships were key.

However, Rochambeau was distinctly unimpressed by the state in which he found the American army, which was much smaller and in much poorer condition than he had been led to believe. Likewise, the number of soldiers in the French expeditionary force was far smaller than Washington had hoped for. Washington was forced to put aside thoughts of recapturing New York and focus on the danger posed by the British from the south. Washington feared that British naval forces would abandon Charleston and travel north to invade along the Hudson River; his fears were exacerbated by the news that a new fleet of 70 British ships had just reached New York. The principle American fortress along the Hudson was West Point, the site on which the American military training academy would later be built.

Washington had placed West Point under the command of Benedict Arnold by Arnold's own request in 1799. Arnold had a reputation as a bold man of action, and Washington had initially offered to place him in a command where he would see action, but Arnold had pleaded that his lame leg made him unfit to ride a horse. Washington later admitted that he had thought it strange for Arnold to wish for such a retired command so far from the front lines, but had agreed to his request anyway.

Unbeknownst to Washington, Arnold had been conducting separate communications with the British for some time. In exchange for a sizable cash reward and a commission in the British army, he had agreed to hand West Point over to them. To some extent, Arnold's motivations can only be guessed at, but it is known that while he was governor of Philadelphia he had spent a great deal of time in the company of Loyalists, or Americans who supported the British. Perhaps more significantly, he had married a woman twenty years his junior who was the daughter of a prominent Loyalist, and who may have been involved in a romantic relationship with British officer and spymaster John Andre. The Arnolds also fell into considerable debt during their residence in Philadelphia, which may have increased the financial incentive for treachery. It was with Peggy Arnold's friend Andre that Arnold liaised for the purpose of passing intelligence to General Henry Clinton.

Because Washington was so anxious that the British would attempt to take West Point, he had written numerous letters to Arnold instructing him to construct extra fortifications there. Arnold had replied with detailed descriptions of all the improvements he was making to West Point's defenses, claiming that hundreds of men were continually at work on the project. In reality, Arnold made had made a slight show of complying with Washington's order by assigning a few dozen men to minor repairs; the bulk of

Arnold's workforce was actually assigned to projects that weakened West Point's defenses considerably.

Washington, along with his aides, made a trip in September of 1780 to meet personally with Arnold and examine the defenses of West Point for himself. Washington arrived at Arnold's home to find him absent; Arnold's aide informed Washington that he had hurried from home that morning in response to an urgent summons from West Point. The summons was actually a warning, letting Arnold know that, the previous night, John Andre had been arrested and searched by American soldiers, who found a number of documents hidden in his stockings. The soldiers did not understand the importance of the documents, but sent them along to Washington anyway. Washington had received the papers, but had not read them before setting out to Arnold's home. Washington and his men rode on to West Point, expecting to see Arnold there; instead, Washington found that none of

Arnold's men had any idea where he was. More shockingly, he discovered that Arnold had been lying to him about rebuilding the fort's defenses.

Washington returned to Arnold's home deeply confused by Arnold's behavior, but not yet suspecting him of betrayal. It was there that Hamilton showed him the papers which had been recovered from John Andre: they included letters written by Arnold containing exact intelligence about West Point's defenses, minutes from one of Washington's own war councils, and a pass issued by Arnold to "John Anderson", giving him safe passage through American lines.

Washington was crushed by this discovery of Arnold's treachery. From someone such as Horatio Gates or Charles Lee, who had always attempted to undermine him, he might have been better prepared for such betrayal, but as far as Washington had been concerned, he and Arnold had always been on excellent terms.

Washington attempted to have Arnold captured and arrested, but Arnold had already reached the safety of the British lines. John Andre, on the other hand, was in his power, and Washington was determined to make an example of him. There was some debate as to whether Andre should be hanged or shot. The first method of execution was reserved for criminals and spies; the second was considered a gentlemanly end to an officer's life. As Andre was a charming, well educated, genteel young man, there was strong feeling among the American officers that he should be given a gentleman's death. Washington, instead, had him publicly hanged, and changed his orders regarding Arnold. Initially, he had wanted Arnold captured; now, Washington ordered him shot on sight.

In an interesting aside, Benedict Arnold's wife Peggy, whom scholars now believe was an instrumental part of the plot, managed to convince Washington, Lafayette, and Hamilton that not only was she entirely innocent of participating in it, but that she had gone temporarily insane on learning of her husband's role. So thoroughly did she deceive them that Washington ordered special safe conduct for her on her journey to her father's house. Later, she confided in a friend how she had pulled the wool over the men's eyes. That friend, the wife of a British officer, later married Aaron Burr, who would be Vice President under Thomas Jefferson.

The Battle of Yorktown

"[George Washington] had done something unprecedented by cobbling together a creditable fighting force from the poor, the young, the black, and the downtrodden, and he had done it in the face of unprecedented political obstacles."

Ron Chernow, *Washington: A Life*

Over the winter of 1780-1781, the American army once again faced a massive shortage of provisions, similar to the excruciating conditions they had faced in Valley Forge three years before. The American economy had long been facing a hyperinflation crisis, due to the fact that the states were printing money to cover their debts. As a result, only British currency had value; American money was worth approximately 3 cents to the dollar, scarcely more than the paper it was printed on. Infuriated by the fact that they were effectively being left to starve by a Congress that couldn't manage national finances, many soldiers broke into outright mutinies—not rebellions, as they remained loyal to the American cause, but demonstrations against what they saw as cruel indifference by Congress to their suffering. Washington urged members of Congress to seek a large loan from France, without which, he believed, the American army would be unable to fight another day. To Washington's relief, the loan was given in March of 1781.

Washington's plans for the last six years had all centered around recapturing New York. But in 1781, General Henry Clinton had managed to waylay one of Washington's letters, which named New York as his primary military target; Clinton responded by withdrawing so many troops to the city that it became virtually impregnable. But Washington was soon distracted by far happier news: from the West Indies, a fleet of twenty nine French ships and 3200 men was sailing to Chesapeake Bay to assist the American cause. The arrival of the French fleet, under the command of the Comte de Grasse, was just precipitated by another piece of excellent news: Lieutenant General Lord Cornwallis, commander of the British army in the south, had retreated with his men to a place called Yorktown, in Virginia. This general location was well known to Washington; it was a peninsula in Chesapeake Bay intercepting two major rivers, which meant that it could be surrounded and cut off from the water. Washington seemed to sense the enormous victory that lay in the American army's future; he was anxious for weeks waiting for de Grasse and his ships to arrive, and when at last they met face to face, Washington reportedly was waiting for them, grinning and waving his hat. Given how reserved Washington generally was, this demonstration of joyous enthusiasm was as touching as it was unexpected. And, considering the outcome of the Battle of Yorktown, it is possible that this was the moment at which Washington first began to realize that an American victory in the war was on the horizon.

Washington feared an intelligence breach that would alert the British to the fact that he had switched his focus from New York to Virginia in time for General Clinton to send reinforcements to Cornwallis. Consequently, he created evidence of fake troop movements, which were so successful in convincing Clinton that an attack on New York was imminent that when Cornwallis realized the danger he was in and wrote to Clinton asking for assistance, Clinton told him the men could not be spared. Even American soldiers were subject to Washington's cautious deception; prior to their long and difficult march from Rhode Island to Virginia, they were not informed of their destination.

Washington and the French commanders planned the siege of Yorktown from Washington's own home, Mount Vernon. This short visit marked the first time Washington had laid eyes on his home since the start of the war in 1775. When Washington left Mount Vernon for Williamsburg a few days later, he was accompanied by his stepson, Jacky Custis, now 27 years old and eager for a stint of belated war service as one of Washington's aides.

When the combined French and American forces at last surrounded Yorktown, they amounted to nearly 19,000 men, while Cornwallis had only 9000 to defend his position. On September 30, 1781, Yorktown was defended by ten redoubts, or fortifications of packed earth standing just outside the British front lines. After more than a week of intense bombardments from canons and artillery, the American and French trenches had advanced close enough to two of these redoubts to hazard a direct assault. The assaults were led by the Marquis de Lafayette and Alexander Hamilton, respectively. Both were captured, which allowed the French and American soldiers to fire directly into the British camp. Cornwallis, sensing defeat, ordered the retreat of a small number of his men, assisted by Banastre Tarleton, but was forced to recall them as his numbers depleted.

On October 17, 1781, after nearly three weeks of fighting, a British messenger bearing a white flag of truce approached the American lines, bearing a message from Cornwallis to Washington which requested a cessation of hostilities so the two commanders could discuss the terms of the British surrender. Washington agreed, and the terms were agreed upon fairly quickly, though

Washington refused to allow Cornwallis's forces to retreat with their colors flying, in retaliation for the similarly disrespectful treatment surrendering American forces had received from the British after the Battle of Charleston.

While the war did not come to an immediate conclusion after the surrender at Yorktown, the war was over in all but name. America sovereignty was shortly to be officially recognized by the Dutch; the Whig opposition in Parliament was adamantly against financing the fighting any longer, despite George III's adamant insistence. Washington did not realize it at the time, but Yorktown was the final significant land battle of the American Revolution.

During his brief time in the camps, Jacky Custis, the last surviving child of Martha Washington's first marriage, caught camp fever. He survived long enough to see the surrender of the British, but he died a short time later. Though Washington had not enjoyed an easy relationship with his stepson, he was reportedly deeply affected by his death. George and Martha would go on to adopt two of Jacky's four children, and raise them as their own. Though their own marriage produced no offspring, in the years after the war the Washington home was always full of children—nieces, nephews, grandchildren, and the children of their friends.

Chapter Six: Building the New Nation 1781-1789

Independence and New Government

"The moderation and virtue of a single character...probably prevented this revolution from being closed, as most others have been, by a subversion of that liberty it was intended to establish."

Extract from a letter sent by Thomas Jefferson to George Washington

"It [has] pleased the Divine Providence to dispose the hearts of the most serene and most potent Prince George the Third, by the grace of God, king of Great Britain, France, and Ireland, defender of the faith, duke of Brunswick and Lunebourg, arch-treasurer and prince elector of the Holy Roman Empire etc., and of the United States of America, to forget all past misunderstandings and differences that have unhappily interrupted the good correspondence and friendship which they mutually wish to restore..."

Excerpt, Treaty of Paris, 1783

One of the most mind-boggling aspects of the American Revolution is the fact that the founders of this strange new experiment in statecraft set out on their quest for political autonomy without having any clear idea what they were going to do with it once they got it. No distinct plan for a particular form of government had been agreed upon. Each state had a governor and a legislative body to run its own affairs, but America—not yet the United States—had only a Congress weakly banded together by the Articles of Confederation, a document establishing cooperation between the states, but which in effect authorized them to do little more than run up debts on the country's behalf. Congress had no way to fund a national treasury except by receiving money from the states, but the states were doing a poor job collecting taxes. This boded ill for the future of the young republic.

Between 1781 and 1783 the fighting had devolved into minor skirmishes arising here and there as a result of natural tensions between the two armies; some 26,000 British troops remained in America, while Washington had to plead with the states not to disband their militias. The financial misconduct of Congress provoked a major crisis in 1783 in the form of the Newburgh Mutiny, as officers demanded their pay, which they had not received for most of the war. An impassioned personal plea from Washington quelled the rebellion, but the need for a strong central government with the authority to take action was all the more firmly impressed upon him.

On September 3, 1783, the Treaty of Paris, or Peace of Paris, marked an official end to the American Revolution. George III's envoys gave approval to all the terms the Americans insisted upon, most important of which was the official recognition of Britain that America was free and independent of British rule. Two months later, Washington disbanded the Continental army, and a month after that, just before Christmas, Washington resigned his commission.

It is difficult to completely impress upon the modern reader just how extraordinary an act Washington's resignation as the head of the army was. In the eighteenth century, it was accepted that whoever controlled the armies controlled the government. There was no other person in the country remotely like Washington, and Europeans took it as given that once the American nation had pulled itself together, Washington would be in charge of it. At least one young army officer had utterly appalled Washington by writing to him with the suggestion that Washington should be instated at the head of a new American monarchy; Washington felt such a strong need to distance himself from this view that he replied to the letter immediately and asked his secretary for proof that the reply had been posted.

Washington's correspondence during the war demonstrates a keen awareness that he had been endowed with an extraordinary amount of power, which in the hands of another person could easily be abused; but because he believed deeply in the essential principle of republican government, that the army must be subject to civilian authority, he made a point of bowing to the directions of Congress, even when their judgment proved not to be in the best interests of the army. The fact that Washington evidently wished nothing more for himself after the war than to return to Mount Vernon and focus on caring for his now long-neglected plantation made him seem more virtuous than was strictly human, in the eyes of the world.

This excerpt from Washington's resignation speech to Congress on December 23, 1783, reveals something of his state of mind as he contemplated a return to private life:

"Happy in the confirmation of our Independence and Sovereignty, and pleased with the opportunity afforded the United States of becoming a respectable Nation, I resign with satisfaction the Appointment I accepted with diffidence. A diffidence in my abilities to accomplish so arduous a task, which however was superseded by a confidence in the rectitude of our Cause, the support of the supreme Power of the Union, and the patronage of Heaven. The Successful termination of the War has verified the most sanguine expectations, and my gratitude for the interposition of Providence, and the assistance I have received from my Countrymen, encreases with every review of the momentous Contest."

Washington delivered this speech in tears, and his delivery moved Congress to tears of their own.

The Private Gentleman Again

As ardently as Washington wished to retire to the peaceful private life of a prosperous Virginia planter once again, the world was not content to leave him alone. Mount Vernon had suffered considerably from his being unable to directly oversee its administration during the nine years he was away at war, and Washington returned home a considerably poorer man than when he left. His time, however, had to be divided between looking after his estate and many less agreeable pursuits.

Washington found himself uncomfortably famous—by far the most famous person in America—and because of this, Mount Vernon saw an almost nonstop stream of visitors who came to lay eyes on the renowned general for themselves. Some of these visitors were Washington's long time friends, appearing either with or without an explicit invitation. Others were complete strangers. Washington felt duty bound to offer each person who presented him or herself at his doorstep Mount Vernon's best hospitality, but the financial strain of looking after so many guests was considerable, to say nothing of the personal aggravation which the reserved Washington suffered from having to make small talk with so many people.

Shay's Rebellion and Return to Political Life

There was a strong feeling in Europe that the experiment in republican nation building that was the new United States could not endure for very long before toppling into anarchy. Washington was deeply aware of this attitude, and found it mortifying. As the 1780s wore on, he became increasingly distressed by the fact that the country was failing to pay any of its loans, lacked a stable hard currency, and had not yet established a standing army or navy. To Washington's mind, as long as America remained a confederation of sovereign states, it would remain a weak, immature country.

Though Washington longed to enjoy his retirement in peace, he couldn't shake his fears or his sense of responsibility to strengthen the nation he had helped to found.

These problems were brought into stark relief by Shay's Rebellion in Massachusetts in 1786, in which a group of farmers who had lost almost everything in the war took radical exception to the state's attempt at taxing them. While the rebellion was short lived and did not have much popular support, it frightened Washington badly, conjuring as it did the specter of a civil war that would destroy the country as soon as it began. He became convinced that the Articles of Confederation should be revised and the role of the central government strengthened. For this reason, and because of the relentless urgings of his army friends such as Henry Knox, he found it impossible to refuse when he was nominated to head the Virginia delegation to the new Constitutional Convention in 1787.

Constitutional Convention in Philadelphia

"The executive Power shall be vested in a President of the United States of America. He shall hold his Office during the Term of four Years, and, together with the Vice President, chosen for the same Term, be elected, as follows..."

Article II, Section I, Constitution of the United States

George Washington's being chose to head the Virginia delegation at the Constitutional Convention is perhaps the one aspect of his involvement in the affair that owed more to tradition than to Washington's new found fame. As we have discussed, he had been an experienced Virginia legislator before the war, and he was part of the original Virginia delegation to the Continental Congress. All of these factors compounded his reasons for being unable to refuse the responsibility given to him.

No business could be conducted at the Convention without a minimum of 7 state delegations being present, which meant that Washington got little work done on the first day, as only the Virginians and the Pennsylvania delegation had arrived at the appointed time. The stated purpose of the Convention was to revise the weak Articles of Confederation, but many delegates, Alexander Hamilton chief among them, came with the intention of outlining an entirely new form of government. Washington was elected the president of the Convention by a unanimous vote, which enabled him to sit and listen and make judgments based on the arguments presented to him. As Washington hated making speeches, this style of participation suited him well.

James Madison, who was the largest slaveholder in Virginia and a member of the delegation with Washington, used the time before the other delegations showed up to craft the Virginia Plan, the blueprint for a national government on which the Constitution came to be based. Gradually, the delegates eked out the design for a government with three branches, executive, judiciary, and legislative, with the legislative branch divided into an upper and a lower house, the Senate and the House of Representatives. This plan contained certain specific alterations to the government formed by the Articles of Confederation, which gave the head of the executive branch less power than Congress itself, which was held to be responsible for its inefficiency. One of the chief sources of debate over the Constitution related to how to fairly calculate the population and resources of states to ensure that they would be proportionally represented in the House. This led to the notorious "Three-Fifths Compromise", which estimated population size by counting slaves as "three-fifths of a man". There was also some debate regarding how the President would be elected, and whether the office should be inhabited by one person or divided between three. Since it was feared that direct election of the President would result in the people only voting for candidates from their state, making it impossible for any candidate to get a majority, the electoral college was instituted.

Nine out of thirteen states were required to ratify the Constitution before it became the official law of the land, though in the end it was ratified by every state except Rhode Island. Ratification by the ninth state, New Hampshire, took place in June of 1788.

The Presidential Election of 1788-1789

Washington's behavior in the run up to the election of 1788 reflected his politically astute yet genuine modesty at the Constitutional Convention of 1775. Once again, he was being considered for an office of immense power and importance, and once again he felt obliged to act as if he wasn't the least bit interested. His reticence to be away from Mount Vernon again for any length of time was probably unfeigned;

his personal finances were suffering so considerably by 1788 that he was obligated to take out a loan just to pay his taxes. Leaving his farms to the care of an overseer undoubtedly cost him a great deal of anxiety.

The new government of the new nation could not do without him, however. Critics of the Constitution of the United States had long taken issue with the section that outlines executive powers. The powers reserved to the President are broad and far reaching, a fact which has created trouble for other new democracies that model their constitution on the American one. The reason executive powers were defined so broadly, however, was because everyone knew Washington was the only viable candidate for the office; the Presidency had been designed with him in mind, and with the expectation that after his election, the precedents he had set would shape the office for his successors. Alexander Hamilton pointed these factors out to Washington in his letters, and further expressed the opinion that the new government was likely to fail if Washington didn't take the office. Washington probably could not have been induced to accept the Presidency if his friends had not made the strong argument that he was duty bound to do so, and that the government couldn't get along without him. Nonetheless, Washington refused to leave Mount Vernon for the then-capital city of New York, or set up his executive mansion, until the votes had been tallied and a message sent to Virginia to let him know the election results.

Washington told Thomas Jefferson that his intention was to serve for only two years, just long enough to set some useful precedents for the next candidates, and then return home again. As it turned out, he served two full terms of eight years in total—roughly the same amount of time he had spent as the head of the Continental army, which in itself had been a de facto head of state role.

Chapter Seven: The First American President 1789-1797

Washington's First Presidential Term

"I dwell on this prospect with every satisfaction which an ardent love for my Country can inspire: since there is no truth more thoroughly established, than that there exists in the economy and course of nature, an indissoluble union between virtue and happiness, between duty and advantage, between the genuine maxims of an honest and magnanimous policy, and the solid rewards of public prosperity and felicity: Since we ought to be no less persuaded that the propitious smiles of Heaven, can never be expected on a nation that disregards the eternal rules of order and right, which Heaven itself has ordained: And since the preservation of the sacred fire of liberty, and the destiny of the Republican model of Government, are justly considered as, perhaps as staked, on the experiment entrusted to the hands of the American people."

Excerpt, First Inaugural Address, April 30, 1789

Washington was and remains the only president ever to be unanimously elected by the American electoral college. Yet even this remarkable display of approbation by his peers was eclipsed by the ceremonies and celebrations that dogged every step of Washington's journey from Mount Vernon to the temporary U.S. capital of New York. Washington evidently found the fuss and grandeur greatly annoying, but perceived that they could not be dispensed with; as a friend pointed out to him, he was a king under a different name now, and royal spectacles came with the job.

During the first year of Washington's presidency, he encountered the same problem he had faced at Mount Vernon, which was that he was continually besieged by guests. Visitors took up so much of his time in the beginning that he was obliged to set specific hours for receiving them. While dropping in at the White House and expecting to see the President sounds bizarre in the 21st century, there was no set protocol for interacting with the President until Washington created some. For instance, the first presidential title and form of address proposed by the Senate was "His Highness, the President of the United States, and Protector of Their Liberties." Washington, who was highly aware that he was being closely watched in case he began to develop European style monarchial pretensions, shunned this recommendation and adopted the simple title, "President of the United States."

The French Revolution

"And I do hereby also make known, that whatsoever of the citizens of the United States shall render himself liable to punishment or forfeiture under the law of nations, by committing, aiding, or abetting hostilities against any of the said Powers, or by carrying to any of them those articles which are deemed contraband by the modern usage of nations, will not receive the protection of the United States, against such punishment or forfeiture; and further, that I have given instructions to those officers, to whom it belongs, to cause prosecutions to be instituted against all persons, who shall, within the cognizance of the courts of the United States, violate the law of nations, with respect to the Powers at war, or any of them."

Excerpt, Proclamation of Neutrality, April 22, 1793

One of Washington's first orders of business after taking office was to create the various departments of the executive branch. He, like presidents since, had the power to nominate the heads of each departments; unlike modern presidents, he had no difficulty getting his appointments confirmed by Congress. Henry Knox, Washington's faithful subordinate during the war, was named Secretary of War (the position that would later be called Secretary of

Defense.) To Alexander Hamilton, Washington's bright, prodigiously talented wartime chief of staff, went the post of Secretary of the Treasury. And Thomas Jefferson, who was still in France at the time of his appointment, serving as the official American emissary to the court of Versailles, was given the post of Secretary of State, though he would not make it back to the United States until 1790.

One of the first major challenges to American foreign policy appeared in the form of the French Revolution and the subsequent wars between the French Republic and Britain. France and the United States were under defensive treaties that had been drawn up during the American Revolution. However, these treaties did not require American aid in the event of an offensive war; furthermore, they had been formed with France's monarchial government, which had since been overturned by revolutionary forces.

Washington opened a cabinet debate on the

subject of whether or not the United States should make a formal declaration of neutrality in response to the conflict; there was no realistic expectation that America, with a standing army of only 3000 soldiers, could involve itself in another war against Britain. Thomas Jefferson was opposed to making an official neutrality statement, perhaps because of secret sympathy with the French rebellion, which might take the defection of their republican allies to heart. Alexander Hamilton, however, insisted on an immediate declaration of neutrality to safeguard America from being preemptively attacked on suspicion of coming to France's aid. This annoyed Jefferson, who would eventually resign from his position as Secretary of State and found the first official political party to opposite the policies of Hamilton and Washington.

Alexander Hamilton and the National Debt

"From this constant necessity of

borrowing and buying dear, it is easy to conceive how immensely the expenses of a nation, in a course of time, will be augmented by an unsound state of the public credit."

Excerpt, *Report on Public Credit*, January 14, 1790

In October of 1789, Alexander Hamilton was asked by Congress to make a plan for addressing the enormous debt the young republic had already saddled itself with, and in January of 1790, Hamilton obliged them with a document entitled *Report on Public Credit*. Longer and far more complicated than Congress had been in any way anticipating, the report proposed a new financial system, modeled somewhat on the British one, which promised to pay off the national debt little by little over a period of years, using a new national income generated by tax revenue. Tax collection fell under Hamilton's purview as Treasury secretary, and he was vigilant in pursuing those who attempted to evade tax duties—in fact, the first function of the U.S. Coast Guard, which was founded by

Hamilton, was to establish lighthouses and chase down smugglers who were attempting to avoid being charged tax when they sold their goods.

Tax collection was a sensitive topic; thus far, taxes were collected within the states, who then passed money on to Congress to fund the national treasury. Under Hamilton's system, however, the federal government would assume responsibility for repaying the debts owed by the states; this would give the government the authority to then tax the states in order to facilitate debt repayment.

Thomas Jefferson, who opposed Hamilton's plan bitterly on the grounds that it took away too much authority from the states, believed that, because Washington wasn't skilled in understanding the complexities of financial systems, Hamilton had pulled the wool over his eyes and turned his own private agenda into national policy with Washington's blessing. But historians are of the opinion that even though

Washington wasn't well versed in financial theory, he and Hamilton shared a nearly identical vision of strong central government for the new nation, and that he understood quite well what the effects would be.

James Madison, long time friend and ally to both Washington and Hamilton, made an irrevocable political split with them both over the debt issue, and Congress itself divided into for and against factions, with the northern states supporting Hamilton's plan and the southern states opposing it. Washington was deeply grieved, not only over the personal split with Madison, but by the introduction of political schism in the American system. It would turn into one of the greatest regrets of Washington's presidency.

The Nation's New Capital

"...a district of territory, not exceeding ten miles square, to be located as hereafter on the river

Potomac, at some place between the mouths of the Eastern Branch and Connogochegue, be, and the same is hereby accepted for the seat of the permanent government of the United States."

Excerpt, Residency Act, March 3, 1791

The first capital city of America was Philadelphia, site of the Continental Congress and the signing of the Declaration of Independence. Philadelphia served as the capital until after the war, apart from a brief period when the British were in control of the city, during which the Congress moved to York, Pennsylvania.

New York became the capital after the war, as soon as the British evacuated it, and it was in New York that Washington lived while he was president. However, Washington, and a number of other influential southerners, advocated for moving the capital to the general vicinity of the Potomac river. Though his reasons for this may seem fairly obvious, he was motivated by more than homesickness. The Potomac lay in the center of the thirteen states, neither too far north nor too far south, with temperate weather and access to the western frontier, which, Washington correctly predicted, would be the chief site of American expansion in the future. Additionally, southern Congressmen such as Jefferson and Madison, who feared that the northern states were growing too powerful, would be mollified if the seat of American power lay closer to their own homes.

According to legend, a deal was struck between Madison and Hamilton over a dinner arranged by Jefferson, to whom Hamilton had appealed for help in solving the problem of growing disunity between the northern and southern factions. In exchange for support for his financial plan from Madison and Jefferson, Hamilton agreed to try to persuade the Pennsylvania Congressional delegation to support moving the capital to the Potomac. It was a controversial plan, and neither side was entirely satisfied. The Federalists in the north believed that Madison, Jefferson, and Washington had engineered the move in order to boost the value of the extensive land tracts they owned in the Potomac region. Madison and Jefferson, on the other hand, came to believe that they had made a bad bargain with Hamilton, as the financial plan he had devised would ensure that the seat of financial power in the country remained with the securities traders on Wall Street in New York. However, it was agreed that the capital should remove to Philadelphia for a period of ten years while the new capital, Washington City, was constructed on a tract of land donated from both Maryland and Virginia. George Washington himself would be out of office before the location transfer took place, but he believed the country would benefit in the future.

The Whiskey Rebellion

"And whereas, by a law of the United

States entitled "An act to provide for calling forth the militia to execute the laws of the Union, suppress insurrections, and repel invasions," it is enacted that whenever the laws of the United States shall be opposed or the execution thereof obstructed in any state by combinations too powerful to be suppressed by the ordinary course of judicial proceedings or by the powers vested in the marshals by that act, the same being notified by an associate justice or the district judge, it shall be lawful for the President of the United States to call forth the militia of such state to suppress such combinations and to cause the laws to be duly executed."

Excerpt from Whiskey Rebellion Proclamation, August 11 1794

The first attempt by the new federal government in 1792 to levy taxes on products manufactured in America led to a rebellion during Washington's first term in office, known as the Whiskey Rebellion. A tax on whiskey had been proposed by Alexander Hamilton in an effort to raise more revenue to pay down the national debt. (Previously, the taxes collected came mostly from foreign and imported goods.) The tax was also seen as a means of strengthening the authority of the central government—federal regulation of whiskey and spirits was seen as integral to marshaling control of some of the country's most valuable domestic products.

A violent uprising in western Pennsylvania ensued, where the tax struck hard at the pocketbooks of poor farmers who distilled most of their grain harvests into whiskey because they could not afford to transport it east for sale. Washington, deeply alarmed, attempted to disperse the rebellion through messages urging the Pennsylvania farmers to lay down their arms and bow to the authority of the new government. A group of four hundred rebels set fire to the home of the tax collector in the area; Hamilton responded by urging Washington to quell the revolt through force of arms. Washington himself led a militia of almost 13,000 soldiers to Pennsylvania to put the rebellion down, but by the time he arrived, the rebels had got word of the size of the forces headed their way; they went into hiding, never to stir against the government again. (The whiskey tax, however, was overturned in 1802 when Thomas Jefferson became president.) Washington remains the only American president who ever led troops into a combat situation.

Re-election and Second Term

Despite the fact that Washington took up the office of the Presidency with the plan of resigning after two years, literally no one else in the government was willing to let him go, even after he had served for four. In fact, as Washington discovered when he began to plan his departure at the end of his first time, most people in the country assumed that he would continue to be president until his death. But Washington had suffered no less than three severe illnesses during his first term, at least one of which nearly killed him, and he was of the considered opinion that his mental resources were failing him, leaving him unfit to fulfill the functions of his office.

Washington went so far with his plans to resign as to ask James Madison to help him draft a farewell address. At this point, however, the factionalism in the American government was at a fever pitch of dramatic tension. Hamilton and John Adams stood with the Federalists on the one side (though Hamilton and Adams bitterly disliked each other), while Jefferson and Madison had created their own Republican party to oppose them. The Republicans believed that the inevitable result of strengthening the control of the federal government would be a reversion to monarchy; the fact that Hamilton modeled the plans for the first national American bank on the charter of the Bank of England scarcely helped this perception. The Federalists saw the Republicans as little better than separatists who were determined to divide the country between north and south. Once again, Washington's unique status as a Virginian southerner who supported strong central government made him the sole force binding these two sides together. Both Hamilton and Jefferson agreed that if Washington left office after only one term, the government would collapse under the bitter feuding of the two political parties.

Washington spent a great deal of time in conversation with both Hamilton and Jefferson, attempting to find common ground they could stand upon, but it was to no avail. Wearily, looking upon another four years in office more as an unwanted duty than as a gratifying thing for his ego, Washington stood for re-election and once again received one hundred percent of the electoral college votes. He was sworn in on February 13, 1793.

Jay's Treaty

"His Britannick Majesty and the United States of America, being desirous by a Treaty of Amity, Commerce and Navigation to terminate their Differences in such a manner, as without reference to the Merits of Their respective Complaints and Pretensions, may be the best calculated to produce mutual satisfaction and good understanding: And also to regulate the Commerce and Navigation between Their respective Countries, Territories and People, in such a manner as to render the same reciprocally beneficial and satisfactory."

From the Preamble to the Jay Treaty, 1794

Washington's second term in office was beset with thorny foreign policy issues, many of which were related to the outbreak of the French Revolution. The Revolution was hailed by Republicans such as Jefferson and Madison as the right and natural effect of democracy's spread across the ocean from America to Europe. They seemed to feel that the bloodshed of the

Terror, in which thousands of French people were publicly beheaded by the guillotine, including the king and queen, was a small price to pay for the overthrow of a monarchial system. Jefferson went so far as to express the opinion that the world would be better off even if that revolution were infinitely bloodier.

As the new French Republic was at war with Britain, Washington sent the first Chief Justice of the United States Supreme Court, John Jay, on a diplomatic mission to England to look into the unresolved issues that remained between the two countries. America still had a number of debts to Britain outstanding from before the war, and the British were refusing to comply with certain provisions of the Treaty of Paris until the debts were paid. The potential breakdown of relations with Britain threatened American merchants, who continued to rely heavily on trade with Britain; but the British were willing to enter into discussions in order to prevent the complication of the Americans being drawn into the war on the side of France. The outstanding issues between Britain and America were sufficiently antagonizing that war seemed certain to break out between them in the near future if they were not addressed.

While in England, Jay negotiated the terms of a treaty with Britain which addressed the evacuation of British soldiers from forts in the western frontier, the exact position of the boundary between America and Canada, and trade with the West Indies. British warships were attacking American merchant vessels and forcing the sailors on them to serve the British navy, claiming that the Americans were deserters from the royal navy. And merchants in the American south were demanding compensation for the slaves the British had freed in exchange for their fighting in British regiments.

The British agreed to all the terms of the treaty, except for those regarding the impressment issue and the issue of compensation for slave owners.

Impressment would not come to a stop until the War of 1812, and Jay, a staunch abolitionist, is thought to simply not have been strongly motivated to pursue the issue of reparations.

The Jay Treaty was the source of incredible controversy in Washington's already divided cabinet. Alexander Hamilton had a strong influence on the formation of the treaty's terms—Washington and Hamilton both believed strongly that the honor and credit of the United States depended on its paying their debts like any other nation. The Republican opposition led by Jefferson and Madison, however, saw no reason to pay more money to Britain, particularly when it would only be used to fund the war with France, the nation which Jefferson still considered to be America's most important ally. The treaty was ultimately ratified by the necessary 2/3rds majority, but it only intensified the divisions in Washington's cabinet.

George Washington Lafayette

In 1795, Washington's personal affections clashed with his public duties when Lafayette's son, George Washington Lafayette, came to America. The elder Lafayette had been imprisoned since shortly after the French Revolution, and while his wife Adrienne had escaped beheading because of American intervention, her life in France was very difficult. George Lafayette had come to the United States expressly to ask Washington to intercede for his father, whose health was suffering from poor jail conditions. Washington, though deeply distressed by Lafayette's plight, faced a quandary: condemned as Lafayette was by the French republican government, any official notice which the American president took of his son might damage diplomatic relations between the two countries.

Washington's short term solution was to offer to send Lafayette the younger to Harvard, covering all his fees and expenses, but the boy declined the offer, too concerned for his father to concentrate on an education. Washington instead wrote to recommend that Alexander Hamilton invite him for a long visit in New York. Washington continued to mull the potential political repercussions of clashing with France over Lafayette's fate, until Hamilton recommended he invite the boy for a visit. Washington chose to receive him publicly. As soon as young Lafayette arrived, he made an impassioned plea to Washington for his father that moved Washington so deeply he immediately wrote to the king of Austria, where Lafayette was imprisoned, and begged for his release as a personal favor.

At the end of Washington's second term in office, George Lafayette accompanied the now former president and his family back to Mount Vernon. Two years later, in 1798, Lafayette's son returned to Europe to see his father, who had finally been released from prison and reunited with his wife and family.

Last Years of Washington's Second Term

Washington's second term took an immense strain upon his health and peace of mind. The lack of unity in his cabinet and the inability of the two parties to set aside their differences and find common ground to meet on had resounding consequences in society and the newspapers. Washington faced criticism of his administration and false reporting about his conduct and decisions in circulars and gazettes. There were times when he bitterly resented having allowed himself to be persuaded to seek a second term in office. This bitterness was only compounded by the fact that Thomas Jefferson, on whom he had relied as a loyal advisor for many years, was so repulsed by having to work with Alexander Hamilton that he resigned from his position as Secretary of State. Washington was overheard to remark that he would quite have liked to resign as well, had he not thought it his duty to stay in office.

The problem lay in the fact that Jefferson and his fellow Republicans were genuinely convinced that Hamilton and his Federalist colleagues had deceived Washington about their true political purpose, which Jefferson believed was to convert the country from a republic to a monarchy. In Jefferson's thinking, that was the Federalist's motivation for consolidating power to the federal government and the executive branch. Jefferson was so convinced that Hamilton wished to revert to a monarchy that Washington became convinced he was borderline delusional. Washington felt unable to trust Jefferson after realizing the depth of his conviction on this matter. By 1795, Jefferson, Hamilton, and Secretary of War Henry Knox had all resigned from their posts, depriving Washington of the assistance of the talented, handpicked public servants whose great abilities and trustworthiness had eased the burdens of the Presidency for most of his term in office.

The heated debate and turmoil surrounding the Jay Treaty had created such a fraught political climate that Washington suffered terribly from attacks in the press, written by strangers and former friends alike. He had never wanted to be president for a second term, and he was achingly eager to return to Mount Vernon, but he had reservations about resigning. There was, as yet, no limit to the number of terms a president could serve, and many Federalists continued to hope that Washington would remain president until his death. But the once enormous popularity Washington had enjoyed had dwindled considerably, and since the Jay Treaty, there was no longer any certainty that Washington would be elected unanimously in his third term.

It was his very lack of guaranteed success in a future election that made Washington fearful of resigning; he was afraid that people would believe that he was only stepping down because his vanity was hurt by anything less than universal acclaim. In the end, on the advice of his most trusted colleagues, including Hamilton (who continued to advise Washington on crucial matters despite having resigned his post) Washington chose to defer announcing his resignation until September of 1796, before the next round of elections but past the point at which any new crisis might arise that would last until the following year.

Resignation and Farewell Address

"Though, in reviewing the incidents of my administration, I am unconscious of intentional error, I am nevertheless too sensible of my defects not to think it probable that I may have committed many errors. Whatever they may be, I fervently beseech the Almighty to avert or mitigate the evils to which they may tend. I shall also carry with me the hope, that my Country will never cease to view them with indulgence; and that, after forty-five years of my life dedicated to its service with an upright zeal, the faults of incompetent abilities will be consigned to oblivion, as myself must soon be to the mansions of rest...I anticipate with pleasing expectation that retreat, in which I promise myself to realize, without alloy, the sweet enjoyment of partaking, in the midst of my fellow-citizens, the benign influence of good laws under a free government, the ever favorite object of my heart, and the happy reward, as I trust, of our mutual cares, labors, and dangers."

Extract, Farewell Address of George Washington, September 17, 1796

Washington had been so set on resigning at the end of his first term that he went so far as to write a farewell statement, or rather, ask James Madison to write one for him. By 1796, however, he no longer considered Madison a friend, and thus it was to Alexander Hamilton he turned to summarize his incredible political career.

Washington and Hamilton worked together to

produce the Farewell Address, with Hamilton composing and Washington making notes and editorial requests. The address was framed as a letter to the American people, and as such, Washington wanted it to speak to the ongoing Federalist versus Republican conflict of his own day, while simultaneously addressing general principles of government that would be relevant to future generations.

The Farewell Address did more than communicate Washington's hopes for the future of the United States; it came to be considered one of the most important articulations of government policy ever written, and its influence on future administrations was considerable. It addressed Washington's concerns about factionalism and ideological divisions, and Constitutional issues such as separation of powers, as well as developing American economic policy and foreign policy. It concluded with sentiments that had Washington had given expression to over and over at each stage of his military and political career: namely, the conviction that his abilities had not necessarily been equal to the tasks he had been entrusted with, but that love for his country and his own profound sense of duty had impelled him to accept these responsibilities and do his best with them.

Washington handed his address over to a trusted newspaper in September of 1796, and with his intentions thus declared to the world, completed the last months of his presidency in a whirlwind of farewell ceremonies and dinner parties, which he attempted to balance with the mountain of legislative paperwork put before him by Congress—bills which had been passed but not yet officially approved and signed by the president, the last necessary step before they became law. Just as when Washington voluntarily resigned his commission as the head of the Continental army rather than clinging to power for his own gain, his stepping down as head of state stunned European observers. No less a person than George III of England remarked that such behavior made Washington "the greatest character of his age."

The example that Washington set in choosing to voluntarily and peacefully relinquish power and become a private citizen again after twenty years as the most powerful man in the country set a powerful precedent for future generations. It was practically a new thing in the history of the world; the peaceful transfer of power from one ruler to the next was thought of as only being achievable through inheritance in a royal family line. (It was, in fact, taken so much for granted that a powerful leader would seek to transfer their power to their own children that Washington's not having any biological children of his own was one reason he was considered a safe and trustworthy choice for first president.)

The third American presidential election took place from November 4 to December 7 of 1796; John Adams was sworn in as the second

American president on March 4, 1797, with Thomas Jefferson, the runner up, as his vice president. Adams later remarked to his wife Abigail that, during the ceremony, Washington looked serene, happy, and deeply relieved to be passing the burden of power to another person. Washington made his official farewell to Congress, then Adams made his acceptance speech. Then, Washington astonished onlookers by stepping back and insisting the new President Adams precede him from the room, an important symbolic gesture which reinforced the essential principle of American politics—that the president, no matter how powerful, was "the servant of the people", a private citizen called to serve for a time and then return to private life.

The precedents Washington set during the end of his second term in his office created such a powerful and enduring legacy that no American president would serve more than two terms until Franklin Roosevelt during the second World War. After Franklin, the 22nd amendment to the

Constitution was implemented in 1951, making the two term restriction law rather than tradition.

Chapter Eight: The Mansions of Rest 1797-1799

Mount Vernon At Last

"Grandpapa is very well, and has already turned farmer again."

From a letter written by Nelly Custis

George Washington returned to Mount Vernon accompanied by his wife Martha, his granddaughter Nelly Custis, and by George Washington Lafayette and his tutor, as well as Martha's pet dog and Nelly's pet parrot. George and Martha both were elated and relieved to be returning to their home at last. The Washingtons had their work cut out for them back at Mount Vernon; just as when George had returned home from the war, he found that the house and the farms had sunk into great disrepair, and needed many expensive repairs. And for Martha's part, the same steady stream of visitors, gawkers, veterans, and old friends that had appeared on their door stop to lay eyes on the old General soon presented themselves in order to catch a glimpse of the retired President. But these were cares and troubles that the Washingtons were happy to exchange for the cares and troubles of George's military and political career.

Among the repairs that Washington planned to make to his house and grounds was a small house, set aside specially just to contain the more than 30 cases of papers he had amassed during the war and the presidency. Later presidents would oversee the construction of presidential libraries, built in their honor to house all the records pertaining to their career. Washington did not live long enough to build his own library, but the incredible effort he expended over the course of his career to see that his papers survived battle and trips covering hundreds of miles of distance demonstrates his awareness that history would have its eyes on him. Many times over his life when Washington came into conflict with someone who questioned his reasoning or integrity regarding a certain issue, Washington shared his preserved correspondences to prove that he had nothing to hide; he seemed to feel that his best defense against any criticism that history might level at him was to make his letters open to the perusal of future scholars and historians, whose power to make or break the reputation of great men he very much respected.

The Quasi War

No sooner had John Adams become president than diplomatic relations between the United States and France abruptly worsened. American ships in the Atlantic were not only being harassed by the British, who were impressing their sailors; French ships also were using the war with Britain as an excuse to board American ships and steal any cargo deemed to be British in origin. Adams sent a diplomatic envoy of three American politicians to France to negotiate the situation with the republican government. The diplomats were not permitted to meet with Talleyrand, the French foreign minister, until they had both paid a personal bribe to Talleyrand and offered a cash loan to France, which they refused to do.

Adams responded by making the United States ready for a potential war: he created a provisional army of 10,000 men and founded the American navy. And because Adams had no real experience in military matters, he wished to give control of the army to Washington, who still had more military experience than anyone else. Through an intermediary, Washington expressed that he would be willing to take charge of the army under two conditions: one, that he would not have to leave Mount Vernon and take the field to prepare the armies himself unless the threatened war with France actually broke out, and two, that he be permitted to choose his own generals, men whom he trusted to get the army into an adequate state of readiness without relying on his direct supervision.

Washington had been following the rise of French-American hostilities closely since leaving office. When Lafayette wrote to him with news of his release in 1798, and a proposal to move to Virginia and buy a farm near Mount Vernon, Washington was forced to write back and tell him that there was so much anti-French feeling in the country just then that he was unlikely to find much of a welcome in the United States. Whatever his feelings for Lafayette, Washington was incensed by the behavior of the French, and of the Republicans in Congress who continued to favor France. Feeling that the country needed him, he was once more unable to turn down the call of duty; however, he was considerably taken aback when Adams announced his appointment as commander in chief to the newspapers without writing to ask or confirm his acceptance.

Washington had sent word to Adams, through an intermediary, that he wanted Hamilton for his second in command; of all his subordinates from the war, it was Hamilton he trusted to prepare the army as he would wish them prepared. Adams, however, had an intense personal dislike for Hamilton and refused to agree to name him to such a high rank at first, though eventually he conceded. However, the provisional army would be disbanded within two years, as ongoing diplomatic relations with France diminished popular support for war.

Washington's Will

"Upon the decease of my wife, it is my Will & desire that all the Slaves which I hold in my own right, shall receive their freedom. To emancipate them during her life, would, tho' earnestly wished by me, be attended with such insuperable difficulties on account of their intermixture by Marriages with the dower Negroes, as to excite the most painful sensations, if not disagreeable consequences from the latter, while both descriptions are in the occupancy of the same Proprietor; it not being in my power...to manumit them. And whereas among those who will receive freedom according to this devise, there may be some, who from old age or bodily infirmities, and others who on account of their infancy, that will be unable to support themselves; it is my Will and desire that all who come under the first & second description shall be comfortably cloathed & fed by my heirs while they live; and that such of the latter description as have no parents living, or if living are unable, or unwilling to provide for them, shall be bound by the Court until they shall arrive at the age of twenty five years; and in cases where no record can be produced, whereby their ages can be ascertained, the judgment of the Court, upon its own view of the subject, shall be adequate and final. The Negros thus bound, are (by their Masters or Mistresses) to be taught to read & write; and to be brought up to some useful occupation, agreeably to the Laws of the Commonwealth of Virginia, providing for the support of Orphan and other poor Children."

Washington continued to take an eager interest in political affairs—the post arrived three times a week, with bulging bags full of letters and newspapers and pamphlets to keep him up to date. His antipathy to Jefferson and the Republicans had only intensified over time, and he made a point of advising government figures like Hamilton, not to preserve unity, as he had urged during his own administration, but to keep a sharp eye on those who would seek to destabilize the new government through Republican political agendas.

But it was domestic matters that took up the chief part of his time and attention in the last year of his life. With his financial situation worsening, Washington began to consider ways to disentangle himself from slavery in a way that would satisfy his conscience without jeopardizing his farm. Like many of the Founders, Washington had come to develop an intense intellectual revulsion for slavery over the decades, but when challenged by committed abolitionists like Lafayette to take serious strides towards dismantling the system, Washington had always balked. His fear of antagonizing slave owning southern politicians whose cooperation he needed had restrained him, as well as his fear that granting freedom to any of his slaves, or allowing them to mingle with free blacks, would antagonize the others, had made a moral coward out of him in this as in no other aspect of his life. But as he grew older, Washington grew increasingly eager to, as historian Ron Chernow puts it, "free himself of the burden of keeping other human beings in bondage."

The famous provision of Washington's will, ordering the freedom of his slaves at his death, was the result. Completed in July of 1799, only five months before his death, the will was twenty nine pages long. Washington composed it in the utmost secrecy, without consulting the advice of a lawyer. Interestingly, even after drafting this will, he kept the copy of the will he made in 1775 before taking command of the Continental army. Hours before his death, he had both wills brought to him in bed, and ordered the 1775 copy burned before his eyes; it has been speculated that this was because he feared that his relatives would seize on any excuse not to carry out his orders regarding his slaves, or else that he himself had not absolutely made up his mind to commit to their freedom until he lay on his death bed.

Only about half of the slaves at Mount Vernon were Washington's to free if he chose. The other half were entailed in the Custis estate that Martha had inherited from her first husband, and would legally pass to Martha's grandson George Washington Custis when she died. Since many of Washington's slaves were married to the dower slaves, Washington knew they would be forced into a painful dilemma, and his unwillingness to deal with that situation prevented him from releasing them during his lifetime. Sensible of the fact that slaves who were given freedom suddenly would have difficulty making their way in the world, Washington set aside funds in his will to feed and house the children and the elderly, and made provisions for the children to be taught to read and write and taught a trade so that they could earn a living. Only one of his slaves, Billy Lee, the valet who was by his side at every moment of the Revolutionary War, was freed and given a pension at the time of Washington's death.

Washington's will was published in pamphlet form and circulated around the country after his death. His decision to free his slaves was extraordinary for a wealthy plantation owner of his era and social class; it was, in fact, as revolutionary a thing as he had ever done. Many of the Founders were abolitionists in name, but even the most committed ones, such as Alexander Hamilton, put their political goals ahead of their principles—and the abolition of slavery was never politically expedient in their lifetimes. Furthermore, as a poor immigrant to America who married into a wealthy northern family, a person such as Hamilton wasn't in a financial situation that made him dependent on slavery; taking an abolitionist stance posed little personal risk to him. This was also true of most of the Founders who opposed slavery in name. While freeing his slaves after his death could not erase the fact that he had held hundreds of human beings in bondage and profited off their labor over the course of his lifetime, the fact remains that Washington's slave owning peers, such as Madison and Jefferson, would never have dreamed of taking such a measure.

In the end, the slaves freed in Washington's will did not have to wait until Martha Washington's death for their release. After a fire at Mount Vernon, which she suspected of having been set by slaves who wished to hasten their freedom by killing her, Martha freed all the Washington slaves a year after her husband's death.

The Death of George Washington

"Washington died in a manner that befit his life: with grace, dignity, self-possession, and a manifest regard for others. He never yielded to shrieks, hysteria, or unseemly complaints... Washington's final hours must have been hellish, yet he endured them with exemplary composure."

Excerpt, *Washington: A Life,* by Ron Chernow

Washington's lifelong habit, whenever he was resident at Mount Vernon, was to make a daily circuit on horseback of all the farms that comprised his estate, which took him from just after breakfast until about three or four in the afternoon. This was how he gave his personal attention to all of the operations that kept Mount Vernon running, and in his younger days he relished the exercise and activity afforded by the daily ride. By 1799, however, he was sixty eight years old, worn down by the strain of his political career, and not as sure on horseback as he used to be. He began to rely on younger men to help oversee Mount Vernon, but made the ride whenever possible.

On December 12, 1799, Washington made his daily ride of Mount Vernon's farms despite bitterly cold winds, sleet, and snow. When he returned for the mid-day meal, there were guests waiting to eat; rather than forcing them to wait on him, he chose to go straight to dinner without first changing out of his snow-damp clothing. Later that day he began to complain of a sore throat, but the next morning, he went about his work outdoors just as usual. By the evening of the thirteenth, his throat was so sore that he could barely speak.

Around two o'clock in the morning of December 14, Washington woke up in severe pain, having difficulty breathing. Modern medical experts suspect that the cause was due to an infection of the epiglottis, which would explain why he choked when he attempted to swallow and had such difficulty breathing and speaking. Martha wanted to send for a doctor immediately, but he refused to let her get out of bed, as she had only just got over a cold. When a slave named Caroline came in to light the fires a few hours later, the best doctors in the area were summoned to Washington's bed side, including Dr. James Craik, who had served with Washington in the French and Indian War.

In their desperation to save him, Washington's three doctors subjected him to the best medical practices known to eighteenth century medicine: blisters, enemas, induced vomiting, and bleeding. It is estimated that over half of Washington's blood was drained. By 4:30 in the afternoon of December 14, Washington knew that he could not survive much longer, and asked Martha to bring him the two wills in his desk; the 1775 version, he asked her to burn, and gave into her hands the one with the provision for the freedom of the slaves. Washington spoke calmly and comfortingly to the doctors and friends who surrounded his bed, declaring that he was not afraid to die, and thanking them for their help.

Washington died around ten o'clock at night on December 14, 1799. According to his instructions, his body was not interred in the vault at Mount Vernon until he had been dead for three days; the precaution, not uncommon in that age, was to prevent premature burial. He was buried on December 18, and his funeral oration was delivered by Henry Lee, his longtime friend and colleague. Martha Washington did not attend; she lived quietly with her grandson in a small set of rooms in the attic of the Mount Vernon mansion house, sewing and occasionally receiving visitors. She died in 1802.

Conclusion

"First in war, first in peace, and first in the hearts of his countrymen, he was second to none in the humble and endearing scenes of private life: Pious, just, humane, temperate, and sincere; uniform, dignified, and commanding, his example was as edifying to all around him as were the effects of that example lasting. To his equals he was condescending; to his inferiors kind; and to the dear object of his affections exemplarily tender: Correct throughout, vice shuddered in his presence, and virtue always felt his fostering hand; the purity of his private character gave effulgence to his public virtues."

From Henry Lee's funeral oration for
Washington, 1799

The reason that we still remember Washington so fondly at this point in history is probably due to the fact that, whatever his failings and vulnerabilities, he had a strong desire to always do what was right: for this reason, his contemporaries considered him a trustworthy steward of power, which is nearly the highest approbation that politicians are capable of.

Historians agree that Washington, though by no means incompetent as the general of the Continental army, was not an extraordinarily talented military strategist; it is well known that he lost more battles than he won. His gift was his astonishing ability to keep the army together in the face of incredible odds—to inspire men who were dropping dead of disease, exposure, and starvation, who were not receiving pay, and who did not even have clothes to wear, to keep fighting for eight years until their independence was won. Few leaders with that kind of charisma, who are capable of inspiring that kind of loyalty from an army, would dream of voluntarily giving up that army after the war. No one in the history of European politics had done it. But Washington believed strongly in an idea of what America could be: a self-ruled republic in which power was transferred peacefully from one servant of the people to the next. Even today, the peaceful transfer of power is still considered one of the most distinctive and original characteristics of American democracy.

It is difficult to grasp, from our modern perspective, just how fragile America was at the end of the Revolutionary War, or how much opportunity there was for the early republic to miscarry. A new nation had been created, but no one was in charge of it. If George Washington had not been such a blatantly obvious candidate for the position of the country's first head of state, if he had not been considered so universally trustworthy, and if he had not been so absolutely committed to doing his duty with no thought for the money or power he could have extorted from his position, it is difficult to say what the result might have been. Unity has never been the defining feature of politics in the United States of America—except in the first few years of its existence, when everyone decided to put

George Washington in charge. The unprecedented unity he inspired was absolutely necessary in order for the country to define itself, resist the interference of foreign powers, and design a system of government that would endure for generations to come.

When one considers the difficulties that faced the country at its inception, the mythology that sprang up around George Washington, beginning immediately after his death, seems almost understandable: the obstacles he faced were so monumental that it is tempting to believe that only a person who was more than human could have overcome them.

Shortly after Washington's death, a biography of him was written and published by a Parson Weems, an Episcopal minister who had made a career of cranking out poorly researched books. He was the originator of the stories about Washington chopping down a cherry tree as a boy, flinging a coin across the Rappahannock river, and beseeching God on his knees for the lives of his soldiers at Valley Forge. Other biographers, though less inclined to make up stories from thin air, did not tend to write about Washington's foibles or quirks, his vulnerabilities, his humor, or his weaknesses. For this reason, the image of Washington that was handed down to posterity was encased in marble, metaphorically speaking, long before the Washington monument was built.

One of the greatest losses that we suffer from having only this soft focus image of Washington transmitted to us is that even though Washington's blessing or disapproval is often invoked by modern politicians for their own agendas, Americans lack a strong cultural understanding of what the father of their country stood for. He worked hard to create the image of a strong leader who rose above factionalism and partisan divisions, but internally, he came to be a committed Federalist who strongly opposed the small government, slave holding, state's rights viewpoints of Jefferson and Madison's Republican party. He believed in taxes, non-interventionist foreign policy, and strong central government. Rarely are these things mentioned in connection with him today.

In regarding Washington as a paragon or a saint, we also lose the sense that extraordinary deeds are accomplished by ordinary people. It is less inspiring to believe that there has never been a person like Washington before or since in all of history than it is to remember that Washington wanted to be remembered. He did not want power for venal reasons, but he did want to improve upon the circumstances into which he was born and rise above his station. In other words, Washington was not born a hero—but he became one because he worked hard, from the time he was a boy, to make himself into a person with useful skills, a finely honed sense of courtesy towards others, a deep sense of duty, and an eye for opportunities to advance his career. Washington was an ongoing self-constructed project. Self-improvement was important to him. He never entirely vanquished his insecurity over his lack of a college education, but he used it to fuel his reading and acquisition of knowledge.

Washington was ill at ease in the company of strangers, but he found it much easier to relax in the company of women, especially his younger female relatives. As a boy, he practiced his handwriting until it was so legible that historians today remark on how easy it is to read. He had severe life-long dental problems, exacerbated by a habit of cracking nuts with his teeth. And though he was famously reserved and made an effort not to show his emotions in public, he felt things deeply, and was prone to tears during tense or highly charged moments. In other words, he was a flawed and vulnerable human being who established an extraordinary legacy through great personal sacrifice. America would not be the nation it is today without him, but he was, first and foremost, a man: one who strived to be great, but above all, one who strived.

Primary Sources and Texts Referenced

Chernow, Ron. *Washington: A Life.*

Principles of Civility
http://www.foundationsmag.com/civility.html

Letter from Governor Dinwiddie to the French
Commander of the Ohio Country
http://explorepahistory.com/odocument.php?do
cId=1-4-1A

The Journal of Major George Washington
http://digitalcommons.unl.edu/cgi/viewcontent.
cgi?article=1033&context=etas

Stamp Act of 1763
http://www.ushistory.org/declaration/related/st
ampact.htm

Declaration of Independence
http://www.archives.gov/exhibits/charters/decl
aration_transcript.html

Treaty of Paris
http://avalon.law.yale.edu/eighteenth_century/
paris.asp

Complete Text of the Constitution of the United
States
http://constitutionus.com/

George Washington's First Inaugural Address
http://www.archives.gov/exhibits/american_ori
ginals/inaugtxt.html

Whiskey Rebellion Proclamation
http://www.earlyamerica.com/milestone-
events/whiskey-rebellion-proclamation/

First Report on Public Credit, by Alexander
Hamilton
http://www.schillerinstitute.org/economy/2015
/hamilton-
first_report_on_the_public_credit.pdf

Proclamation of Neutrality
http://avalon.law.yale.edu/eighteenth_century/
neutra93.asp

Residency Act
http://memory.loc.gov/cgi-
bin/ampage?collId=llsl&fileName=001/llsl001.d
b&recNum=253

Last Will and Testament of George Washington
http://founders.archives.gov/documents/Washi
ngton/06-04-02-0404-0001

Made in the USA
San Bernardino, CA
02 February 2017